Inside Creative Writing

Inside Creative Writing

Interviews with Contemporary Writers

Edited by

Graeme Harper

Professor and Director of the Honors College, Oakland University

First published 2012 by
PALGRAVE MACMILLAN

Palgrave Macmillan in the UK is an imprint of Macmillan Publishers Limited,
registered in England, company number 785998, of Houndmills, Basingstoke,
Hampshire RG21 6XS.

Palgrave Macmillan in the US is a division of St Martin's Press LLC,
175 Fifth Avenue, New York, NY 10010.

Palgrave Macmillan is the global academic imprint of the above companies
and has companies and representatives throughout the world.

Palgrave® and Macmillan® are registered trademarks in the United States,
the United Kingdom, Europe and other countries.

ISBN: 978–0–230–21217–6 paperback

This book is printed on paper suitable for recycling and made from fully
managed and sustained forest sources. Logging, pulping and manufacturing
processes are expected to conform to the environmental regulations of the
country of origin.

A catalogue record for this book is available from the British Library.

A catalog record for this book is available from the Library of Congress.

10 9 8 7 6 5 4 3 2 1
21 20 19 18 17 16 15 14 13 12

Printed in China

Contents

Acknowledgements

Sincere thanks to all the fabulous writers here, who kindly answered these questions. Without you nothing could have been done to explore these things. Your friendliness, and your willingness to respond, has made this book. Thank you so much. Acknowledgement is also made of the assistance of A P Watt on behalf of Philip Pullman and Nadine Gordimer; Mic Cheetham on behalf of Iain Banks; and Barbara Mobbs on behalf of Kate Grenville. Thank you, one and all! Needless to say, many of the writers in this book have websites containing further information on their works (I've noted a couple of these websites at the end of this book – but I'm pleased to recommend a visit to all). Thanks to the reviewers of the final manuscript of *Inside Creative Writing*. Your support was a timely, and wonderful, encouragement. To Kate Haines, and to Jenna Steventon at Palgrave Macmillan: my tremendous, heartfelt thanks to you both. Thank you for your vision, your support and your constant good humour. Thanks also to Felicity Noble and the rest of the Palgrave team. Finally, and with much love always, to Louise, Myles and Tyler: here, a book full of creative writers – a wondrous thing!

About the Author

Graeme Harper is Editor-in-Chief of *New Writing: The International Journal for the Practice and Theory of Creative Writing*, a Professor of Creative Writing, and Director of the Honors College at Oakland University, Michigan. He has held the post of Professor of Creative Writing in the UK, USA and Australia, and was inaugural chair of the Higher Education Committee at the UK's National Association of Writers in Education. His books include *On Creative Writing* (2010), *Research Methods in Creative Writing* (2012), edited with J. Kroll; and, writing as Brooke Biaz, such works as *Moon Dance* (2008), *Welcome to the Communion Islands* (2010) and *The Invention of Medicine* (2012).

Introduction

Creative writing

This is not a book primarily about works of literature, film, theatre or otherwise. These are terms most often used in relation to the *completed* works of creative writers, works that are publicly the result of the activities of creative writing. These completed works (and the experiences they bring to readers and audiences) are absolutely worth celebrating. However, creative writing does not begin with these works: creative writing does not begin where it ends.

Creative writing does not begin when a creative writer has released one work or another into the public sphere, if ever these works are released into the public sphere. Creative writing begins, and is largely undertaken, in the realm of the individual, even if that individual is collaborating with other individuals. Creative writing begins with ideas, emotions, understandings and a *desire to do it*, that is located in the someone, or in 'someones', who have that desire. Creative writing is, in this sense, a decidedly human event, an activity that is driven by our urge to create.

This book is about that human activity of creative writing – the act of doing it, and the knowledge that underpins the acts and actions of creative writers who are, or have been, doing it. The reason for this is straightforward. Have you ever encountered one of those books in which someone who has read a creative writer's work asks them a range of questions about that work? Something along these lines:

'So, in XXXX you explore the nature of what it is to be YYYY?' And the creative writer replies something along the lines of 'Yes, I wanted to explore YYYY. It's something I've been interested in for quite some time.' Or, alternatively they reply: 'I'm not sure I do explore YYYY, actually. I think of XXXX as more of an exploration of AAAA.'

There is nothing fundamentally wrong with this kind of information, or this approach to discussing works of creative writing. Equally, it might not matter, and critics of literature might well suggest that it *does* not matter, whether the creative writer is incorporated into the interpretative loop of all this or not. It's possible and laudable to approach a work of creative writing and respond to it. Read into and through it and even in some sense *write* it. And to do this by a response that occurs *post-event* (that is after the originating events of creative writing). A creative writer – whether fiction writer, poet, screenwriter, new media writer, playwright or otherwise – often has many very interesting things to say about their complete, public works and sometimes, in exactly the kinds of books that explore those works, they can provide some wonderful recollections of how those works were made, harking back to the *event* of creative writing while themselves engaging in some post-event considerations, memories, thoughts, even new speculations.

But, of course, the greatest amount of time a creative writer spends is that concerned with beginning their work, developing their work, considering and re-considering incomplete work. Along with this, thinking or speculating on future work, re-considering work-in-progress. This includes wondering what idea or emotion or intention might produce a new piece of creative writing, or develop one already in motion. While most of these activities are in pursuit of finishing something, some time, they are not finished in themselves, or even all so plainly connected with a 'macro' result (such as the completion of a novel or the completion of a poem) that the 'micro' elements (singular choices of technique, individual thoughts, emotional sparks) have a direct or obvious connection with finished work. Creative writers spend much of their time in moments, and in modes of perception, memory, and (sometimes wild!) speculation. Without such activities creative writing wouldn't occur. Yet the ability to approach these moments, *post-event*, or to discuss these through the evidence available in the public realm, is relatively low.

How, then, do we come to understand creative writing? How do we improve our own understanding and knowledge of it, as creative writers? How, also, do we share knowledge about creative writing between those who do it, and with those who enjoy the public results of doing it, even if they don't do it themselves? We can, and we surely will, go on celebrating and exploring and enjoying the publicly distributed works of creative writers. Creative writing as an art form and as a form of communication brings us so much, as individuals and as groups, cultures and societies. Completed works have a role in our societies in extending the ways in which human beings relate to each other and enjoy the world. *Undertaking* creative writing equally brings us so very much. What we seek through further consideration of creative writing is what lies within our undertaking of it, and how we might further engage with what is undoubtedly a significant human activity.

Fifteen questions, fourteen writers

The fifteen questions that are the focus of this book came from a personal consideration of some of the creative writing ideas and actions that felt pressing to me. These are the writers I asked to answer these questions:

- Iain Banks
- Charles Baxter
- Andy Brown
- Maggie Butt
- Jack Epps Jr.
- Nadine Gordimer
- Kate Grenville
- Nessa O'Mahony
- Ruth Padel
- Robert Pinsky
- Philip Pullman
- Tom Shapcott
- William Tremblay
- Xu Xi

Short biographies of these creative writers are included at the end of this book. More than one of these writers will be very well known to readers – indeed, these are creative writers who have published widely, won some of the world's most important literary prizes, taught creative writing to many students, had famous films made of their books, written a famous film or two as well, and generally been publicly visible.

However, it was decided at the outset not to work on the premise that I would *only* interview those creative writers who were extremely well known to the majority of people in the English-speaking world. This is not intended to be a book about levels of fame, just as it is not a book about the reception of finished works of creative writing. These things are intriguing, often very exciting, and in a great many ways supportive of our celebration of creative writing generally. But these things are not what *Inside Creative Writing* is about.

It *was* decided, however, to include creative writers who have completed some work that has been publicly distributed. The reason for doing this is to acknowledge that creative writing is both art *and* communication between people. So the creative writers included here have all seen their work publicly exchanged, between creative writer and reader, between creative writer and audience. The circumstances differ, the personal circumstances differ, but all these writers have all had some external involvement in their final works, some publishing or producing involvement. This is what holds these creative writers together as a 'set' for the purposes of exploration. In other words, this is a cross-section of creative writers who have had some external distribution of their final works, and who write in English. They can be considered, in that sense, a selection, or a sample, or a case study.

The fifteen questions asked of these writers aim to take our explorations beyond an investigation of finished works. This is not to reject those kinds of books – those books that ask mostly about 'the novel', 'the play', 'the collection of poetry', 'the film'. Those kinds of books will be well known to readers here. But the aim of *Inside Creative Writing* is to ask more about particular *doing* aspects of creative writing itself, particular ways of thinking and acting. The purpose here is to extend how we investigate creative writing and, through a comparative study, explore whether creative writers offer us significant clues to important aspects of creative writing, simply in the way they think about it.

The questions were asked over a period of just over two and a half years. In every case, these questions were presented to the writers in the same manner. You'll notice I have been informal and personal in tone. I felt I was intruding into a personal space, and I wanted to acknowledge that in the tone of my questions. I was also aiming to keep consistency in the manner and method of asking – so I did not vary this tone. As a 'control' approach I presented each question in the same manner: fifteen questions, in the same order, and in the same words. Logistically – after enquiring with each of the creative writers, in turn, asking if I could ask some questions for this book, the questions were sent individually to the writers, via email, and their answers were received the same way.

All the writers except one received the questions this way – that is, via email. Nadine Gordimer received the questions via fax, and returned them the same way. William (Bill) Tremblay received the questions by email and returned them the same way – however, he reworded the questions, or summarised them, no doubt endeavouring to pick up what he felt was the essential core of the question. In his responses I've thus included his rewordings beneath each question.

What follows in each of the chapters of this book is an exploration of the answers given to these questions, a comparative consideration of how these creative writers approached these questions, and an exploratory discussion of what these answers might point us towards.

Nature, nurture and creative writing

Because creative writing is acts and actions[1] it is mobile and fluid. It can be no other way than this – otherwise, it simply would not happen. Alternatively, doesn't our day-to-day use of words, our general use of words, endeavour to be fixed? That is, don't we aim to convey a meaning in words, in our general writing (or, indeed, speaking), that can be exchanged with a high degree of immediate understanding and certainty – between speakers, writers, listeners, readers? Alternatively, doesn't any particular act of creative writing embrace the aim of doing something lively and appealing with words? Might that be an aim that can sometimes unsettle meaning or challenge our immediate understanding?

Absolutely! Acts or actions of creative writing can set out to purposely challenge the role of particular words or expressions as widely agreed signifiers[2] and by doing so works of creative writing can ask the reader, or audience, to re-consider established human meaning or revisit what is shared, in terms of understanding. It is easy to see how attractive this might be, though not necessarily that it might always be comfortable. There's great potential here for new human knowledge – if something is looked at anew there is a chance, perhaps even a very good chance, that something will be discovered, some new insight will be explored and enjoyed. However, that word 'appealing' might also refer to something perhaps slightly less challenging, but just as important.

Activities of creative writing, an arts' practice that uses words as its primary tools, might strengthen how a word, phrase or expression encapsulates an agreed human principle or a human ideal, and it might be that what is sometimes interesting about creative writing – more so than in other modes of written expression – is that creative writing takes a widely agreed word or collection of words and delves further into what these signify for us, so that what is an everyday thought a common feeling, expressed in words, a common place thing, becomes renewed and our interest in it, and knowledge of it, is revitalised.

These are possibilities. In fact, one way of thinking about the tools, the words, that creative writing uses is to think about creative writing as *exploring possibilities with, and through, words*. During creative writing itself, before any public document is realised or released, it is this notion of possibility that harks back in various ways to the perception, memory and speculation in which the creative writer is consciously and subconsciously engaged. Perception, memory and speculation relate directly to how creative writers approach the actions of creative writing.

Words are one site of these actions, one focus of the activities of making that is creative writing; and words are key tools, as well as key components, in the explorations that are undertaken. Therefore, in the event of creative writing the relationship of a creative writer to words is incredibly significant, and we might wonder what it is that draws certain humans to use, or even to *want* to use, words this way. Not everyone wants to be a creative writer or to engage in using words in a way that might highlight or prioritise the kinds of usages for which creative writing is renowned. This includes both challenges to everyday use and delving deeper into what these words might point towards, what they might notate. But, of course, words and exploring the uses of words, is only one element in creative writing, significant though it might be.

Simply put, where do creative writers come from? Does the interest in doing creative writing result from some kind of environmental condition, an exchange of a specific kind, in which a creative writer emerges because of what, where, how or who they encounter? Is it primarily about being drawn to telling stories, using images, constructing intriguing juxtapositions of ideas and expressions, relating observations so that others might share that thing or occurrence with the writer (even though those others may not have observed the same thing or the same occurrence)? Creative writers, distinctive users of words, undertake other acts and actions too; but, indeed, where *does* the creative writer emerge from?

We might well ask: can a creative writer ever emerge from a place in which there are no final pieces of creative writing, completed or otherwise – for example, a home without novels, a place without books of poetry? Not to forget, of course, that creative writing can contribute to all manner of creative results, from books to films, from computer games to plays, from children's picture books to websites, from radio plays to works of design, fine art or music. We might ask, also, does a creative writer only emerge if someone, somewhere, at some time, encourages them to engage in creative writing? Or does this occur from an internal observation, a motivation produced inside ourselves, so that regardless of outside influences something has been triggered that ensures we will at least attempt creative writing, at very least show some interest in doing it. Is this emergence of the creative writer any different to the circumstances that encourage the emergence of other artists, other creative individuals?

Scott Barry Kaufman and James C. Kaufman, in their edited book, *The Psychology of Creative Writing,* bring together a variety of experts, mostly psychologists and educationalists, to offer some fascinating explorations of such things as 'process', 'flow', 'genius', 'physiology', creativity'. In that book, the opening chapter, Jane Piirto's 'The Personalities of Creative Writers', offers a current answer to the above questions:

> Creative people are those who do creative acts. The creativity occurs in the becoming, the making. In the struggle to be creative, personality attributes are extremely important.[3]

Then the editors of *The Psychology of Creative Writing* quite rightly declare that 'we eagerly look forward to future research and debate'.[4] So it is: a need for us to find out more, to explore and discuss and consider creativity more! There are further explorations for us to undertake in order to get closer to some answers, to assist us in understanding how creative writing comes about, and why those of us who do it choose to do it.

We might inquire too: 'Would anyone be prevented from being a creative writer by someone else's assessment that certain attributes of their personality didn't suit them becoming a creative writer? It is hard to imagine this would happen, not least because one element of being engaged in creative writing is human passion, that strong personal yearning to do it. However, there are considerations here related to the nature or nurture of creative writers, whether it is possible to be nurtured as an artist, or whether, indeed, artists are born.

The wonderfully named C.E. Seashore, writing in *The Musical Quarterly* almost one hundred years ago, and speaking about another art form, declared:

> Musical talent probably lends itself better than any other talent to the laws of mental inheritance, for the reason that it does not represent merely a general heightening of the mental powers but it specifically recognised as a gift which can be analysed into its constituent elements, many of which can be isolated and measured with reasonable precision. The inheritance of musical talent may, therefore, be studied, not only for itself, but also for the bearing it has on the inheritance of mental traits in general.[5]

Could the same be said of creative writing – that the ability to undertake it is inherited; that it is mostly, if not simply, a matter of nature? Similarly, writing in the first half of the twentieth century, this time in the *Journal of Educational Sociology*, Edwin Flemming joined the personal with the cultural and suggested that 'for artists and art to survive, our milieu must provide sustenance and encouragement for the development of the artistic personality'.[6] According to this view, it is a case of either having an artistic personality or not having one. Following this view to its conclusion, if you don't have an 'artistic personality' you are unlikely to produce any art of any kind. But even if you do have an 'artistic personality' this is not enough because you require society to support it.

Moving into our twenty-first century, but keeping with the music analogy, we find Michael Pickering and Keith Negus, in an article entitled *Rethinking Creative Genius*, offering a slightly different view:

> ... we argue for the reconceptualisation of creativity as at once ordinary *and* exceptional, involving the links people make between an everyday conception of creative acts and an apprehension of exceptional creative acts. Genius may often be narrated in terms of exceptional moments of musical insight or breakthrough, but these are always firmly embedded in an extended process of arduous toil and preparation before a musician is able to become at one with their art and synthesize from a range of existing cultural elements.[7]

Here creativity is ordinary, something we all possess. Exceptional creative ability is located in genius, but genius can only come about – at least, they say, in the field of music – by embedding in a process of hard work and preparation. In other words, everyone can engage in creative acts, everyone is born with the ability to be creative, but to be exceptional as an artist, to be regarded as having a heightened ability, this involves something more.

In these discussions words like talent, creativity, toil, gift, preparation point us towards questions that are not entirely answered, might never be answered, or might even be unanswerable. These are questions about where the artist – the creative writer in our case – emerges, and how artists (for our purposes, creative writers) might best be supported. Undoubtedly we might then be drawn to ask about the education of creative writers.

It has always been the case that creative writers have combined types of formal education with types of informal education. That is, creative writers have engaged with schools and universities, have entered 'apprenticeships' or mentoring relationships with other writers, editors, publishers, producers; and creative writers have always learnt a great deal of what they know by continuously *doing* creative writing, by the general undertaking of it. In the learning of creative writing a multitude of things can evolve. Such things as ways of viewing the world, ways of expressing a view, ways of moving from thoughts or observations to words, ways of marshalling ideas, ways of engaging with emotions, ways of using the forms and structures of creative writing, ways of working from start to finish of a piece of creative writing, ways of continuing as well as ways of starting a work. In relatively recent years, creative writing has become more widely taught in schools, colleges and universities. In being more frequently taught in these places this way some might say that creative writing has now become *formally* part of education – even if it had been *informally* part of educational environments for many, many centuries. Where we draw the line between the informal and the formal in education is a big question, and one that is somewhat beyond the scope of this book.

But should you take a creative writing class or not; and, if you do take a creative writing class, and are encouraged or discouraged at points during this class, how should you react? What is the relationship between formal avenues of education and informal education in creative writing, and is this relationship evolving somehow, so that what we are seeing in the early twenty-first century are potentially distinctive developments in the history of creative writing as a human practice? Developments such as those involving forms of e-learning, or informal learning via social media, or even new ways of distributing works of creative writing, finished or unfinished.

These are important questions as creative writing grows more popular, and more widespread, more accessible through new technologies that have delivered activities of creative writing, as well as *works* of creative writing (sometimes called the 'artefacts' of creative writing, meaning *objects* that emerge from doing it: books, typescripts and so forth), more directly to people's homes. By works of creative writing I mean, of course, not only those finished works of creative writers that might well have been released to the public, but now also the works of creative writers that emerge during creative writing itself – drafts, communications about those works (emails, for example), complementary works (works that may or may not be creative writing, but that emerge during your creative writing – notes, annotations, suggestions to yourself for future works).

When considering the creative writers interviewed in this book, and their answers to the questions posed here, we can ask ourselves whether their creative writing seems to be contained in their natures, or whether they reveal that it is primarily the result of various types of nurture. Generally speaking, no one has yet fully comprehended such a relationship between nature and nurture. That is the case across all the arts, of course, as well as specifically in relation to creative writing. We can compare the answers of the creative writers in this book and consider how nature and nurture appear to be contributing – say, for example, in different ways for Andy Brown and Kate Grenville, or for Jack Epps Jr. compared to Robert Pinsky, or for Nessa O'Mahony compared to Philip Pullman. Some of the questions in *Inside Creative Writing* also aim to draw out this nature-nurture discussion – Question 2, for example, which…, and Question 8, which is about the places these writers undertake their creative writing.

Creativity, process, environment

What is creativity? Is creativity primarily located in the *results* of our actions? Is it located in the *actions* themselves? Or is it mostly located in our ways of thinking? In our ways of perceiving? And is this the case regardless of the actions or results that come about? Perhaps it is located all three of these. In *The Courage to Create* Rollo May neatly describes creativity as 'the process of bringing something new into being'.[8] This may be a good place to start some thinking, but two complex ideas appear in this definition: firstly, the idea of a *process* and, secondly, the idea of something *new*.

If a process involves a 'series' of actions, as its general definition suggests, then much in creative writing cannot be considered a process; that is, one thing coming after another, a certain kind of chronology, a series. A great deal in creative writing doesn't work that way. Actions and ideas, perceptions and memories, crafting and critical understanding, all intersect in any event of creative writing. This can happen in very individual and project specific ways. To suggest that such activities might always be placed in a series would be to underplay almost every aspect of the unique events with which creative writers are involved. Instead, the kind of thoughts and actions with which creative writers are involved is better considered as syntheses, the coherence of which is contained in the creative writer themselves – as a creative writer, this synthesis is your own way of approaching the acts and actions of creative writing. A creative writer brings about this synthesis, declares the *individual* while, undoubtedly, is in so many ways also representative of the *cultural*.

May's word 'new' is complex, and important enough to us to warrant our consideration. If May means new, as in 'only now discovered' or as in 'only recently found out', then it would be difficult to argue that this is the case for every act of creative writing. Some creative writing is not new, in that sense, even though your own undertaking of it, and the results of that undertaking, might contain elements that are new. However, the themes, the subjects, even some of the ways in which you approach creative writing might be already established. So your undertaking might be considered, more accurately, a *re*newal rather than the bringing into being of something *entirely* new. We could well ask, would this kind of creative writing be any less creative, any less representative of human creativity?

This question is one concerning value and it might not be the value of the actions themselves that is the focus of this valuing of creative writing; rather, it could be the value of the creative writing artefacts emerging, any of which may be valued in a certain way because of prevailing historical conditions at the time of their valuing. Or it could be the value associated with certain ideas about 'originality', a concept that also attaches itself to ideas about creativity. Some commentators have said that 'it is impossible to give a simple definition of creativity'[9]; but, equally, deliberations concerning originality do very little to simplify how we can approach an understanding of exactly what being 'original' might mean. George Bailey offers us this:

> It may be that in concerning ourselves with works of art we engage in a long-standing practice that counts as a genuine achievement someone's being the first person to accomplish anything whatsoever (where 'achievement' imputes virtue to the person whose achievement it is). An account of why this practice exists might attempt to track our development as highly competitive creatures, and might explain our valuing originality in art and artists as a consequence of the value we find in the ability of someone or something to dominate any situation. This value... may well be the basis of the value that originality in art has to people in certain art-making cultures (just those cultures that place special value on a work of art's originality).[10]

So originality, in Bailey's view, is possibly associated with the competitive nature of human kind, involves some kind of 'ability' and some kind of dominance, and in terms of artistic value is related to 'certain art-making cultures' and the idea of what is 'special'.

For those of us interested in where the arts (including creative writing) might originate, all of this is interesting, and certainly alerts us to how discussions of creativity, art making, developing artistic ability, and valuing the public works of artists, is complex and full of many possible interpretations. But, of course, all this doesn't practically get us a great deal closer to what creative writing might involve and, most particularly, just how its undertaking combines human actions and understandings, certain activities and kinds of human knowledge.

Coming to understand more about creative writing, involves exactly that: considering both our actions and the knowledge that informs our actions. Without considering both of these we are unlikely to get much closer to increasing our abilities to engage in creative writing. We are unlikely to get closer to an understanding of how creative writing happens. By concentrating primarily on the actions, but investigating very little about the knowledge behind them we don't get closer to that understanding. By spending almost all of our time investigating the knowledge behind creative writing but very little time exploring the practicalities of the actions we don't get closer to that understanding either. Only by approaching *both* our actions and knowledge behind our actions are we unlikely to get closer to increasing our abilities to engage in creative writing. This includes our understanding of how creative writing happens, what creative writing is, and how creative writing has come to be part of our world, or part of the lives of individual creative writers – ourselves, or others.

1

Beginning Creative Writing

Do you recall when you first thought you might like to write? I mean professionally or, at least, so that others might see what you'd written. Or is it all more of a 'continuum' – in which case, I've started on the wrong question, and I best start back-pedalling!

The question of when, why, how and where creative writers emerge is one of considerable human interest. As with questions about the emergence of other artists, society is interested in knowing the answer to 'where did this activity begin?' Communities are interested. Educationalists are interested. Many other creative writers are interested, comparing these emergences with their own personal histories. Readers and other audiences are interested, in order to locate works of creative writing in the individual lives of the creative writers who have produced them. If we do value having creative writers in our communities, there is always the attached question of whether we can do anything to encourage more of them to emerge and more of them to live around us. So these sorts of questions arise in a general way, but what about the individual creative writer?

What about you, if you have started doing some creative writing or if you've thought about doing some creative writing? Is there something other creative writers might reveal about their writerly beginnings that could assist you in starting out and making your way as a creative writer? That's what this first question in *Inside Creative Writing* aims to investigate.

It's a fact of life that human actions have beginning points and end points. One of the hardest things to decide with creative writing is whether creative writing can be separated from other life activities quite enough for anyone to say when they actually began doing it. For example, do you begin creative writing *only* when you begin to write a poem or a story or a script, or did that writing begin long before anything was ever put 'on paper'? That is, does your creative writing begin when you first have an idea or an emotion that eventually becomes a story or a poem, the core of a script or the narrative of a computer game? Do different forms of creative writing have different kinds of existences in that time before the physical act of creative writing? These are good questions for us to ask ourselves, even if answers are elusive, because such questions alert us to the ways in which creative writing incorporates a wide variety of undertakings, some conscious, some unconscious.

It is likely most people would not be comfortable saying that anyone is doing creative writing unless something is actively, physically being done. So, that good friend who often says 'one day I'm going to write a novel', most of us would feel, is not *actually* engaged in creative writing, even if their imagined novel sounds like it will be wonderful, one day, some day. Creative writing is, by this simple definition about 'doing', a physical act. And therefore it is an initial physical act that tends to be seen as the beginning point of creative writing, even if we are aware that our physical action is preceded (and followed) by a range of our thoughts and emotions.

But creative writing is also something we don't buy off the shelf. By this I mean that you don't need any specific external object to undertake it, something you might see, acquire and learn to use. While most creative writers today will write with some kind of writing device – whether a pencil or a computer or some other instrument – this is not absolutely necessary for creative writing. So, given that much that occurs in creative writing can be invisible, the notion of observing a physical action is not quite as simple as my earlier comment might suggest. You can, for example, compose pieces of creative writing in your head, without any instrument at all – at least in the first instance. Simply then, creative writing uses words, mostly, and it uses them in ways that are often not only about providing information.

If we ask this question about beginnings, and think about that, we might begin to pinpoint a moment when *we* used words in a particular way. It might be that, in this sense, the idea of beginning creative writing relates to doing something distinctive with words. Of course, I have also added to the question asked of the creative writers (as above) an additional element – what we can call 'the element of exchange'.

Do you recall when you first thought you might like to write? I mean professionally or, at least, so that others might see what you'd written. This brings about something else for us to consider. You can, of course, do some creative writing and never show it to anyone. In opposition, it could be said that creative writing is a form of human communication, as well as an art, so not communicating with anyone but yourself creates something of a cul-de-sac – even though the enjoyment you gain from undertaking some creative writing might be reason enough for you to do it.

There are no rules about showing your work to others. There are no laws stating 'you must distribute your creative writing to the world'. However, the question asked of the creative writers here in *Inside Creative Writing* is connected with the idea that these are people who in some way see creative writing as their profession; or, at very least, something they do with some form of human exchange in mind, at some point in their activities. This is not the only way a question about beginnings could have been approached. For example, I could have asked 'when did you feel you could call yourself a "creative writer"?' and perhaps have ended up with quite a range of alternative answers to the ones found here. I could have asked 'what was your first piece of creative writing?' Again, this most likely would have produced quite different answers to the ones we read here. And so on.

Finally, beginnings suggest endings. Someone might be a creative writer from the day they start creative writing until the day they die. Or they might write during a certain period of their life but stop writing afterwards. Creative writing is not necessarily a long-term life choice, and I've hinted at an exploration of that in the question asked of the writers here. For example, the creative writer who writes as a teenager but doesn't return again to creative writing until late adulthood might not consider they had begun creative writing at all for much of their life.

Once again, there are no rules or laws about these things. Likewise, a creative writer might still consider themselves to be engaged in creative writing even if they have finished one project and not yet begun another one. In that sense creative writing could involve a series of beginnings and endings! That said, the creative writers interviewed here do appear to have a long term engagement with creative writing and their beginnings do indeed seem to have produced a relatively constant engagement with creative writing.

As with all the other questions in this book, each writer was asked the same question, and no style, length or structure of answer was suggested to them. Simply, the question was asked as it appears here and the answers were given – with sincere thanks to the writers.

*   *   *

Iain Banks

I was an early developer, or at least aspirationer. I wanted to be a writer from primary school days (I have documentary evidence in the shape of crayon drawing from Primary VII; we were asked to draw what we wanted to be when we grew up and while my pals were all depicting firemen, train drivers and astronauts, I drew a writer. Well, actually I drew an actor, but it says AND WRITER in big white crayon in one corner, so I'm claiming it).

Charles Baxter

This question goes back to the Dark Ages of my own development. It never occurred to me that I might make anything like a respectable income from writing, so I always thought of it (until about ten years ago) as a sideline. As a child, I lived in several imaginary worlds, and in high school I wrote short stories, and then in college, weighed down with emotions as I was, I turned to poetry. After that, and slowly, I turned to narrative fiction. But the idea that I might write professionally seems impossible, outrageous, absurd.

Andy Brown

I think I can say that I've always read and always written, and that I had a strong sense from a very early age that books, writing, and reading *really do matter* to us all, culturally, historically, as well as on a very personal basis. However, I also think that I had very little sense that, when I wrote as a child, I was doing anything other than responding to what my teachers had asked me to do: 'Write me a short story about X', or 'Write me a poem about Y'. I can really only remember one short story I wrote, aged 14, about a dying man and his antique car and something spiritual about the old banger's symbolic, cracked headlamps. My teacher and my parents all seemed to like it a good deal, which gave me the permission to think that my writing might hold some value for others, which is all it's really about in the end. My grandmother, and my mother in her turn, were both avid readers – although my dad never read anything but the *Reader's Digest* – and I think their influence was seminal in my understanding how engaging and powerful the written word could be.

The first time I remember writing anything for myself, because I actually *needed* to write something down, was as a teenager, writing songs for a band. Lyrically, they were very poor – the usual adolescent stuff – but there was a huge amount of energy and commitment behind them. We used to do a lot of gigs and I would regularly receive that all-important audience response. I carried on song writing and slowly discovered more sophisticated subjects. I used to act a good deal too in school productions – we had a fabulous theatre and some amazing, committed staff – and I loved exploring that complex relationship between performance and the written word. I also learned some memorable speeches: the soliloquies from *Hamlet* are still with me 30 years later.

What I most wanted, however, aged 18, was to get away from home. My years at Leeds University were a crucible of creativity: more acting, lots of bands, reading lots of novels and poetry, drawing, painting, and writing lots of songs, poems, stories, travelogues and so forth. I also discovered all the great singer songwriters when I was a student – my roommate put me onto all sorts of new music and onto contemporary poetry too, and I wrote hundreds of poetic songs without the faintest idea of what I was really doing, or how to do it 'properly'. It was all done by intuition. What's perhaps interesting is that I studied science at University – specifically Ecology – and all these creative activities were simply hobbies on the side; something I did whilst my academic, scientific training went on under the tuition of dedicated research scientists.

When I left Leeds, paradoxically, I found myself continuing to work with a band who still lived up there. I, on the other hand, had moved back down to London. I wrote all the lyrics, sent them the words in the post, and they put them to the music. Every couple of months I'd nip up the M1 and do some rehearsing, before going into the studio to record the album. We recorded in New York and the UK, and made three LPs this way (LPs – remember them? Some of them still get played on Radio Helsinki twice a year and I receive a royalties cheque of £6.14 pence). We toured the UK too, supporting some big bands, so the experience was exhilarating and fairly unique. After some time, however, the M1 just became too long for us, the distance too difficult, and I found myself still writing lyrics, but now without a backing band. Which essentially meant that my songs were no longer songs, but poems. I had to decide what I wanted to do about that.

I then fell in love. I mean I *actually* fell in love, and moved to the wilds of the Welsh mountains with the woman whom I would eventually marry; and I also fell in love with the (very real and possible) idea that one could actually *be a poet*. In Wales I wrote poetry seriously for two years. I mean, I *practised* poetry, I read poetry and I talked and lived it with any and everyone who seemed interested. I taught myself how to write poetry 'properly'. I also got maddeningly isolated and developed hill-walker's calves and a beard that was much too long for a 25 year old.

To cut a very long story short, after moving back to London for a year to train as a teacher, and then moving to Exeter to teach in a school, I started sending these poems out to magazine editors. I remember clearly the first acceptance letter coming through the post, and jumping for joy that someone actually wanted to publish what I'd written. From that point on it has just snowballed, in a rather complex, demanding, but highly rewarding way: I guess this is the 'continuum' of which you've asked; from one accepted poem to ten books, it has all just emerged.

Whilst it certainly does emerge, it isn't something that 'just happens'. Save for perhaps one genius in every generation, I firmly believe that 'being a poet' means a great deal of very hard work, and getting involved with the wider writing world: you have to make your own opportunities and generate a bit of luck too. You have to try to live generously and openly with other writers and readers and audiences. Understanding this got me involved early on with organising regional events and festivals and, as a result, my partner and I later landed ourselves jobs as Arvon Centre Directors. It was only whilst running Arvon's writing courses for six years – and I had already published my first book by then – that I experienced what you describe as the 'thought-you-might-like-to-write' moment. After years of doing it, and being involved, I understood that I could perhaps begin to fulfil my ambitions through writing poetry. Twelve years on I'm Directing a creative writing Department at Exeter University: simply doing the writing (trying to make each poem better and different than the last) has given me the privilege of meaningfully exploring the notion that I 'might like to write', both for myself and for others.

Maggie Butt

I was seven when I started collecting neat copies of poems and stories in note-books, and very early I conceived an ambition to be able to write 'poet' in the Occupation section on a passport, when I had my own. By the time I got there, I actually wrote 'Journalist.' Towards the end of my English degree, deciding what to do for a living, I thought, 'The two things I like doing best are writing and talking to people. How can I earn a living doing those?' Journalism seemed like the best answer. Ironically, I found writing poetry and journalism were mutually exclusive activities for me. So writing has certainly been a continuum, an unbroken thread through my life, even though it has been in different forms at different times, sometimes public facing and sometimes intensely private.

Jack Epps Jr.

As a freshman in college I took a class where the assignment was to write in the style of a famous author. I picked Hemingway. The story worked and I was sort of hooked on writing. I took creative writing classes and became an English major. I was reading my way through college. I stumbled onto a small film festival at my school and uttered those fateful words, 'I can do better than that.' I enrolled in a film-making class and have been involved in films ever since.

I made some short films that won some awards and that only fuelled my passion. After graduation, I went to Los Angeles to find my fame and fortune as a director. I started writing as a way to direct on paper. A friend of mine had some connections with a television show, and we sold a teleplay. It was at that point where writing suddenly started to make sense. But I knew my interests and instincts were in feature length films and not television so I began studying the longer form. Once I sold my first feature screenplay, I was pretty much hooked. I had seven unproduced screenplays before I got my first movie made. And that film was TOP GUN. So I went from being an unknown quantity to an overnight sensation. It takes a long time and a lot of hard work to be an overnight sensation.

Nadine Gordimer

When I began to find reading was the most essential activity for me, out-reaching by far my ballet and acrobatic dancing.

Kate Grenville

I've pretty much always wanted to be a writer – at primary school we wrote 'compositions' which these days we'd call 'creative writing' and I churned out many melodramatic stories on such familiar subjects as 'Encounter with a Bear' (a tale of two woodcutters in a forest attacked by a bear – a weird mix of my reading at the time, Robin Hood meets The Last of the Mohicans...). I sent off my first short story when I was about 16 – to a women's magazine which returned the tiniest rejection slip I've ever received. At the end of high school and through university I made several abortive attempts to write a novel. The problem with these early efforts was that I was studying English literature – the towering works of the genre – and could only be disheartened by my own feeble first efforts.

A breakthrough came for me when I happened on the FIRST novel by Virginia Woolf – a writer I hugely admired. It's fairly ordinary, especially by comparison with what she wrote later – and for the first time I realised that great writing doesn't just descend in one burst of genius, it evolves over long periods of time.

The real breakthrough, though, when living in Europe and being exposed for the first time to avant-garde American writing – it offered a way out of the cul-de-sac of the overly-polite, overly-correct 'well-made story' tradition that I'd thought was the only way you could write. I'm quite a 'traditional' writer now, but those Americans (Robert Coover, John Hawkes, Ronald Sukenick etc) allowed me to find my own voice.

Nessa O'Mahony

Like many writers, I suspect, I spent my childhood wanting to write although the stories I retold in my head were ones I'd found in books or in television. I wanted to write stories and poems in school English to impress the teachers I had crushes on, but had the desire educated out of me at university (first-time round), where all the writers we studied were clearly male and dead, which ruled me out. I began my career as a journalist, so was a professional writer, and got an enormous satisfaction out of seeing my by-line under improbable articles about insurance and banking. But it wasn't until I turned 30, and took a creative writing class for the first time, that I got bitten by the bug to be a 'proper' writer. I still remember the thrill of hearing a magazine editor who had accepted one of my stories answering the phone and saying, 'Oh, Nessa O'Mahony, the writer?'

Ruth Padel

I showed my first poem to my mother when I was three, published poems in the school magazine, carried on writing poems off and on while doing a PhD and then more seriously while writing the PhD up as a book. I always read about writers, and felt myself to be one of them, but even after I'd published two or three books I did not think of it in terms of a 'career' – just of doing the writing itself.

Robert Pinsky

In childhood I had fantasies about making music or movies, or painting, or dancing, or acting, or designing cars and household equipment – being an 'artist' though for me at that time and place the word was limited to making pictures. Among those daydreams, writing must have been there, but not pre-eminent.

In high school, I began making a bit of money playing the saxophone at high school dances, in bars, weddings and bar mitzvahs, dances etc. Nothing very glorious, but that was the first ambition to get beyond daydream. In my high school graduating class I was voted 'most musical boy' and without much talent I began aspiring to be a great jazz player.

At Rutgers, just as I was beginning to comprehend my limitations as a musician, I fell in love with poetry. I had great teachers: Paul Fussell for Freshman Composition, and other classes after that. Frances Ferguson, author of *The Idea of a Theater*. And some of my contemporaries at Rutgers have published books: Alan Cheuse and Peter Najarian in fiction, Henry Dumas (who died very early) in poetry.

Philip Pullman

No, I can't remember. There was never an age when I thought I might do anything else – or rather, since I toyed with various other ways of earning a living, such as being a lighthouse keeper or a tramp or a Customs officer (I liked the boats on the Thames in London), there was never a time when I thought that writing wouldn't occupy the most important part of my attention.

Tom Shapcott

Originally I wanted to be a composer, but at age 18 (in 1953) I was called up to do National Service, and I found I could keep a small notebook in my pocket, but not a music score. I started seriously to write (poems). At that stage *The Bulletin* was the only national weekly, and they published a lot of poems. For 2 years I submitted poems to them, and in 1956 had my first poem published. I suppose had I gone to university I might have published in student journals, but I had left school at 15 (not uncommon then; education was only given a major boost by Prime Minister Menzies in the mid-1950s). My first book was published in 1961 and won what was then the only Australian poetry prize, the Grace Leven Award. I was on my way.

William Tremblay

Do you recall when you first thought you might like to write for publication?

I was not suddenly transformed into a writer like Paul struck by lightning. Rather, it has been a persistent need, a jangle in my cells like an addiction to nicotine.

I had written since before high school mostly to clarify my perceptions. Published a few poems in Clark University's literary annual. But it wasn't until my mid-20s that I shared my poetry with a friend who gave me the address of a guy in Minnesota she had met onboard a ship sailing to Norway.

Turns out this was Robert Bly.

The first time we met [1968] in Worcester, Massachusetts, he went through the entire manuscript of what would become my first book, *Crying in the Cheap Seats*, red-penciling the rhetoric from each poem. It was a sea of blood, yet I learned to respect the sensibilities of a reader who prefers implication to statement, connotation to denotation, imagery to explanation. He helped me immeasurably, and I will always be grateful for his generosity.

He appreciated a raw human-based realism in my work, though his own poetics are more toward what some called 'American neo-surrealism.' What is essential to him is the soul. He praises everything that strengthens the soul; he attacks everything that crushes the soul.

My poetics are instrumental. I have a predilection for poetry that makes manifest the presence of an inner life in ordinary experience. I have come to believe it is possible for poetry also to explore questions about language itself. But I also think that it is about *them*, everything or everyone open to be understood, as well as my uncertainty, my sense sometimes of being carried on the 'drunken boat' of language toward unforeseen shores.

After my first book was published I became a professor of creative writing. Waves of aspiring poets have come into my life, each with their own emerging poetics I have tried to help along by shifting from a judgmental to an astonished mode from which they can learn and grow.

Xu Xi

I started very young because I published my first piece at 11 in the children's section of Hong Kong's main English newspaper. They paid in 'honour points' which, if you collected enough, could be exchanged for cash! Now this was extra pocket money to buy Superman & Batman comics (books were WAY too expensive as these were strictly library back in 1965 Hong Kong!) So I sort of always thought that writers published their work, although interestingly, because of my strange linguistic conundrum of writing in English in a Chinese world, I did not think that anyone like me was a 'writer.' I published several more pieces between the ages of 11–13 in that same space but there was no 'teenage section' for writing so after that I just continued to write (by then mostly fiction) and what with the pressures of our public exams and the need to go to university, I didn't think too long and hard about being a writer.

It wasn't till my mid-20s when I finally understood that no matter what the rest of my life was and would be about (and I refer to that time as my terrible 20s) I was always and forever a writer first and foremost. Hasn't changed since then.

* * *

On evidence, childhood plays a considerable role in creative writing beginnings. Almost all the writers interviewed mention the word 'childhood' directly, and those that don't at very least point towards it. While some of this childhood creative writing heralds a future direction rather than necessarily being a 'beginning point' for a creative writing career, there's something in those exploratory ventures into creative writing as a way of expressing an idea or an emotion. It could be that it is not so much the early starting that is the primary thing here but, rather, the openness and exploratory nature of childhood itself that is significant as an encouragement to trying some creative writing.

From there, whatever beginnings childhood offers for creative writers the next element of beginning often relates to some kind of educational setting – although the form of educational setting is not necessarily the same from one creative writer to the next. Colleges or universities are sometimes significant. But more significant, at least at first glance, is the general role of reading, or the role of *having an appreciation of works of Creative Writing*. This is very common. However, what is read – that is exceedingly individual. There's enough here to speculate that a connection between one work of creative writing and one new or emerging creative writer might well be enough to set someone off on a life-time of creative writing. Sometimes other arts – looking here at Tom Shapcott's case in relation to music, for example – provide additional creative outlets and hone connected interests. Then there's that element of confirmation, if that is what it is: the showing, publishing, releasing of pieces of creative writing to a wider audience. Maggie Butt, among others here, mentions such a thing. This releasing doesn't appear to define our beginnings as creative writers, but it certainly features as something of personal and individual significance.

To summarise by drawing from the writers' answers: we begin at a point of openness to exploration, look to some kind of education to assist us in understanding what constitutes a good piece of creative writing, and then we aim to complete something that can be shared with others. Of course, my summary is a generalisation and each creative writer will do these things in their own way. That element of individualism – yours or any other writer's – lies at the heart of why and how we creative writers begin to be creative writers, and to see ourselves this way.

Exercise

Would you consider that you have begun creative writing? If so, why, when and how? If not, why not, and what might you do to begin now? Try writing down the story of your beginnings – your previous ones or your future ones. Titled this 'Beginnings' (suggested word length for this exercise: 300–500 words).

Reflection

Because some kind of reading – in the broadest sense of what reading means – forms part of a creative writer's beginnings, can you remember any pieces of creative writing that have been particularly significant for you? If so, in what ways have they been significant and how do they relate to your own creative writing interests?

If you're interested in creative writing, and it's somewhat of the assumption in this book that you are, what aspects of it are most likely to please you? For example, are you seeking to win a certain literary prize, or are you mostly wishing to express something you have wanted to express? Both perhaps? Is it mostly you you're aiming to satisfy in doing some creative writing, or do you have a someone or someone/s in mind that you'd most like to please by writing something (for example, a reader of a certain kind, or an audience of a certain size or type)? When you begin a piece of creative writing do you ever consider these things?

2
Creative Writers and Others

Would you 'blame' anyone else for you becoming a writer? Obviously, I'm joking about the 'blame'! But I wonder, are there any key figures (real, or imaginary!) that come to mind, especially in your earlier writing career.

Because creative writing is a form of communication, as well as an art, then the immediate consideration becomes what specific people are involved in this communication? Plainly we human beings engage in, and support, the activity of creative writing. But how are particular creative writers encouraged and who encourages them? We've seen already earlier that creative writers can talk of beginnings and of those things that contributed to their pursuit of creative writing.

As humans are relatively social animals, we all would like to consider that the things we do are at least tolerated by our peers, even if the final results of these things don't necessarily become celebrated. Therefore, any encouragement to undertake the things we enjoy must bring us a degree of pleasure. So there's always an element in creative writing that suggests human connections, even if the actions we undertake, and the things we produce, don't even leave our own, personal spaces. Creative writing, in that sense, is never not *some* connection between human beings, never something removed from communication and what might be called 'creative human exchange'.

Add to this the somewhat obvious fact that creative writing uses words and words form languages and languages, whether spoken, written or otherwise, suggest agreements between human beings about commonsense meanings and general understandings. In essence, then, our creative writing *is* connections, our creative writing *is* exchanges and our creative writing *is* about support for other humans. This might sound overly grand, but it is hard to say it is not true, at very least in the sense that to creatively record in a language used by humans, and in a way enjoyed by humans, something that is relevant to humans, adds to our store of understanding and contributes to our sense of what it is to be human – that is it, simply, but importantly, worthy of acknowledgement.

All this could lead to a consideration of how you personally define *success* in creative writing. Because this book has asked questions of published or produced creative writers, it might be expected that a key element of that success is located for the creative writers interviewed in the distribution of completed pieces of creative writing, and those who have supported that. So, as an obvious example, that might be success associated with being published and with those who have assisted and developed a creative writer's publishing history. In this way, the idea of success is defined according to something *beyond* the creative writing itself – in essence, by someone or someones who agree to invest in one or more of your works of creative writing. This investment might happen for reasons that are commercial, cultural, personal or a combination of all these. Such a thing is neither innately good nor innately bad, it is simply a fact.

A supportive relationship between a creative writer and someone who publishes their work can assist the creative writer to continue writing, financially speaking. It can mean the creative writer has to write certain things (*even* if they might like to write others). It can mean the creative writer's work is more widely read than it would otherwise be. Or it can mean that the creative writer has deadlines that either assist or challenge their desire to produce the best work they can possibly produce. The complexity of the relationship between a publisher and a creative writer, or between an editor working at a publishing house and a creative writer, is considerable. It remains today one of the most significant examples of a specialised industrial or cultural conversation associated with creative writing.

The question asked of the creative writers here in this chapter is *not* about professional conversations, necessarily. Nor is it necessarily about success or support. The word 'blame' is used – in a light hearted fashion; but it is easy specifically to refer to the idea that creative writing has at its core creative human exchanges of some kind. But what kind?

One way we might speculate on this is to think about whether those exchanges relate to a type of interchange of imaginations. The philosopher R. G. Collingwood talked of the imagination as having a 'sensuous experience, at its base'.[1] We can consider how imaginative connections initiate forms of support, as well as forms of human exchange that are not purely intellectual in nature. Imaginative exchanges, and the kinds of networks of friends and colleagues that can potentially be part of those exchanges, can be the meeting of sense impressions, and both creative writer and their audiences might benefit from these exchanges of impression. Taking that thought a little further, this could well be related to what has also been called 'creative benefaction',[2] in which the creative writer, and others, confer aid, offer support, create habitats and situations where the creative writer can best undertake their creative writing.

But the question asked of the creative writers here is far less tangled than all that. In its open-endedness – *Would you 'blame' anyone else for you becoming a writer?* – this question was open to the creative writers' individual interpretation.

* * *

Iain Banks

Not really. It's partly an only child thing, maybe; a kind of determined independence. I owe all my English teachers thanks because one and all they encouraged me, and my parents were always supportive, but I wouldn't attempt to pin the responsibility on any one person.

Charles Baxter

No, there's no one to blame. Sometimes I wish there were. I had a curious, secretive family, and that always helps, because the power of unspoken conflict sensitizes anyone who is paying attention. But it's mostly a matter of temperament. When I was sixteen or seventeen years old, I began to read fiction seriously, and I thought, 'I'd like to do that.' Hemingway was inspired at an early age by Jeffery Farnol. For me, the writer whose work did that trick was J. R. Salamanca.

Andy Brown

Yes, as I said before, my roommate at Leeds turned me on to contemporary poetry – Hughes, Plath, Larkin et al. – and we discovered Shelley and Blake together too. And another young poet friend turned me on to other poets – Ashbery, Harwood, and the American and European avant-garde. This poet friend and I had a tempestuous (not entirely friendly) relationship whilst we were both working out what we liked and how we might write our poems. So, thanks to both of these people, I was reading a great deal of poetry before I fully realised that poetry was what I would eventually *do* myself.

I also 'blame' the people who published my early work, much of which seems a real shambles to me now. But, even if I didn't know what I was doing when I wrote my first book, that work did possess a certain energy – a certain *something* – like my old teenage songs. Now, of course, I feel like I'm writing maturely; writing the work I want to; the work *I need to* write. And I hope I do know a little more of what I'm doing these days. That's not false modesty: the process of writing is a continual learning curve and I feel certain I would abandon it if it were not. With this in mind, I also 'blame' the people who encouraged me to pursue my current interests and styles, and might also 'blame' my influences but, seeing as they had no conscious part in encouraging me, it hardly seems to be their fault. Apportioning blame would be churlish: let's face it, there's no one to blame but myself.

Maggie Butt

I suppose I'd have to 'blame' my parents for loving stories and poetry and putting books into my hands.

Anne of Green Gables assured me it was OK to live in the imagination, which was just as well, because I was far more there than in any real world. Elizabeth Barrett Browning and Enid Blyton showed me girls could make a success at it as well as boys.

You sometimes hear stories of young hopefuls who happened to meet an older writer, who guided and encouraged them. I sometimes wonder what might have happened if I'd had a teacher who'd taken an informed interest in my writing, or if I'd been lucky enough to meet a writer who became a mentor. In fact I didn't ever come across anyone who knew about writing or the world of publishing. Perhaps that's why I've ended up teaching writing myself, so that others can have a helping hand, and why I want to see it taught right through the curriculum, and see writers firmly embedded in schools. Having a knowledgeable mentor shouldn't be a matter of privilege or chance.

Jack Epps Jr.

Not really. When I began writing I could only probably name a handful of writers that I admired: David S. Ward, Bill Goldman, Robert Towne, John Milias. I was really influenced by a vast amount of films that I was discovering for the first time: Hawks, Wilder, Ford, Sturges. At that time, if you wanted to see a certain film, you had to work at it – find it at a revival theatre, or stay up late to watch it on television at 3 am. Now I think it's too easy to get access to films. I think a lot of people put off seeing films by saying, 'I'll see that later.' And they never do. I am surprised at how film illiterate most young writers are today. Every young writer should be watching films everyday – and not just contemporary films. Learn to watch films of the '30s and '40s.

Basically, I wanted to make films – and writing was the quickest way to get the film up on the screen. I have a very visual style. I see the film, the scene, the images. I try to capture the movie I am seeing in my mind on paper. I fantasize, free associate and then try to capture the film I am watching in my mind.

Nadine Gordimer

I became a writer as the result of being a reader. There was something for me to explore in the word, perhaps, stories to tell that hadn't all been told. My first 'adult' story was published when I was fifteen and the editor didn't know I was a child – I certainly wasn't telling. A couple of years later, I was 'discovered' by the Africana poet, Uys Krige and his fellow poet and journalist, Charles Eglington, who bravely started an avant-garde literary magazine, also anti-racist.

Kate Grenville

The women's movement in the 1970s was an important source of creative energy for me – it offered an important and new subject (contemporary women's lives and dilemmas) and it offered a new language and culture. My fictional efforts were coloured and informed by reading in feminist writers of the time – both fiction and non-fiction. Germaine Greer's writing was very important because as well as being a brilliant and original thinker she's a great stylist.

Nessa O'Mahony

I suppose I'd 'blame' my first creative writing tutor, who didn't for a moment imagine, when introducing me to the thrills of creative self-expression, that he'd be consigning his solvent, fully-employed career girl student to a future of bohemian insecurity. I could also 'blame' Elinor M. Brent-Dyer (author of *The Chalet School* series), Agatha Christie, Émile Zola, Jane Austen, the Brontës, Patrick Kavanagh, W.B. Yeats and Seamus Heaney, but most of them couldn't fight back so it doesn't seem fair, really.

Ruth Padel

Gerard Manley Hopkins, Virginia Woolf, Katherine Mansfield and Tacitus – the writers who really excited me when I was 17.

Robert Pinsky

No creative writing teacher, but brilliant instructors like Fussell and Ferguson, and also certain lofty or romantic notions of the writer, part of that period. In one way, Richard Elman's biography of Joyce or Yeats's prose; in another, the near-worship of Hemingway and the still-fresh adventure of Kerouac and Ginsberg.

But, with apologies if this is grandiose, it was in me: all through the music period – and earlier, as far back as I can remember – the sounds of words, the insides of words and their cadences, the musculature of sentences: that's what most deeply occupied me, and where I felt most capable.

Philip Pullman

No-one else is to blame. But I don't like the idea of 'becoming a writer', or of 'being a writer'. It smacks uncomfortably of essentialism. Writing is contingent, not essential. Could you say someone was a writer if they didn't actually write anything? That in some mysterious sense they were 'essentially' a writer? I don't think so. Think of those contemptible people – usually men, usually American – who claim that they're 'blocked', and if it weren't for their 'block' they'd have written several masterpieces by now, and who assert a double privilege: that of being esteemed as a 'writer', and that of being regarded with awe for their mysterious and existential suffering. What bollocks. If you can't write, do something else. As for myself, I am much more interested in doing than in being, and I define my activity with a verb and an adverb: sometimes I write.

Tom Shapcott

I lived in isolation in Ipswich, a mining and industrial town, so early influences came from reading. I had no personal mentors, teachers etc. Once I was published things changed and I met other writers. Of these, the most compelling was my close contemporary Rodney Hall, but we had utterly different approaches and styles, which was why we could show each other what we were writing, make comments and criticism without treading on toes; it worked well; certainly for me, though Rodney back then was hardly known. I read voraciously in contemporary poetry, English and American. Once I began to publish I made sure I got acquainted with the work of Australian poets.

William Tremblay

Who were the poets who influenced you most?

In grade school it was the Bible. In high school it was Shakespeare first. We read *The Merchant of Venice, Romeo and Juliet, Macbeth*, and *King Lear*. I found the story of Job in Lear who had the Fool rather than the three 'wretched comforters' as companions. I was thrilled by the beauty of his language, the depth of his understanding of the human heart, the way each character had a leading metaphor, an individual style of speech, and a pretension or mask. Second, it was Walt Whitman who expanded me with his long, comprehensive, embracing line which balanced good and evil, male and female, light and darkness often within an antithesis. Emily Dickinson's hymns surprised me with their open affirmations of even death. Later, in college, it was T.S. Eliot whose poems were emotionally engaging and terribly abstract at the same time. I fell in love with the idea of 'free verse' though I recognized the truth of what Eliot, Pound, and Williams were saying, that free verse does not mean 'no measure.' But what measure, then?

I could blame the waves of rhythm & blues quartets that broke into the public airwaves at mid-twentieth century. It could be that Elvis, Bob Dylan, or even John Lennon are 'to blame'. To be young, to want to 'say something', to enter the social conversation with words of your own devising about what you and everyone you love is going through, is to soar toward the big heat in the sky.

William Blake also has had a formative influence on my thinking.

Others among Modernist poets are Federico García Lorca, Wallace Stevens, Hart Crane, Robert Frost, Dylan Thomas, Sylvia Plath and among 'world poets,' Kabir, Rumi, Li Po, Wang Wei, George Sefaris.

I do not mention my Postmodern contemporaries as it would be very expensive to print all their names. I have written two score reviews and have been positive or silent.

Xu Xi

No not really, because it was just something I started doing quite naturally. The determination not to fail I blame on my mother because she doesn't read, would rather that I had become a doctor (this for the girl who despised biology), and who even wanted me out of the arts.

*   *   *

With a question jovially posed about *blame* we end up with quite a few replies relating to *admiration*. 'Brilliant instructors like Fussell and Ferguson,' answers Robert Pinsky. 'The writers who really excited me when I was 17,' says Ruth Padel. 'William Blake also has had a formative influence on my thinking,' comments William

Tremblay. All revealing admiration of particular creative writers, as well as admiration of particular works of creative writing. What's this all about?

One component of these responses relates to the appreciation of others who can do creative writing well. This might be as simple as the awe that was felt (and later remembered) by a beginning creative writer for the achievements of certain established creative writers and, even more so, for certain works of creative writing that represent a high level of achievement. The well known expression 'having something to aim for' is probably extremely relevant to us here, as is the simple notion that something done well is admirable.

Another notion that has relevance relates to our general human natures, and whether we are in essence competitive creatures who admire others who compete well. So, for example, thinking about the highly accomplished musician and the highly accomplished basketball player produces similar (though not perhaps identical) kinds of responses. It would be difficult to suggest seriously that their accomplishments are in the same vein, but we admire each, and both, nevertheless. You might ask yourself if a competitive streak may be more or less evident in all of us – and even more so if it relates to a particular field of endeavour we admire. However, such an interpretation does mask a spectrum of other values and meanings. For example, do we value sports in the same way as we value the arts? Perhaps, perhaps not. Likewise, how specific might our competitive natures be – would a poet admire a novelist in the same way a novelist would admire another novelist? Perhaps, perhaps not. And does everyone view creative writing as something we 'become'. Philip Pullman's concluding comment 'sometimes I write' presents an interesting alternative way of viewing the activity of creative writing.

That said, parents, other writers, friends, teachers, those presenting certain ideas that seemed important to present: all these receive a mention as contributors to one or other creative writing career. It could also be that admiration and inspiration go hand-in-hand. Psychologists have referred to inspiration as 'a sudden apprehension of the essential nature of a thing.'[3] With this in mind, other works of creative writing represent not only achievement, and not necessarily just points of competitive reference, but apprehension of the essential nature of creative writing as a way of approaching the world and the ideas we each develop within it. 'Hemingway was inspired at an early age by Jeffrey Farnol,' notes Charles Baxter. 'For me, the writer whose work did that trick was J. R. Salamanca'.

To be inspired by another creative writer's work combines aspects drawn from our wider appreciation of the arts as human undertakings, along with the personal ambitions of individual creative writers, and feelings relating to 'the essential nature' of a work or range of works. However, along with the recognition that 'blame' is a playful word, rather than necessarily an accurate description of what is going on here, there's also a strong indication that creative writers take a high degree of personal responsibility for deciding to begin to write, and for continuing to do so.

Exercise

Can you write down any key figures in your life who have influenced your creative writing? Are any of these figures writers? Are they involved in other arts? In what ways are they inspirational? Are there any works of creative writing you would also call 'inspirational'? If so, what do you admire about these works and does that admiration relate to something you are also aiming to achieve? As an exercise do this in point form, to see whether you can break it down to the very basics, to the core of these links (suggested word length for this exercise: 150–200 words)

Reflection

If our personal discoveries about the world influence our decision to begin and continue creative writing, have you made any discoveries that you can immediately pinpoint as significant for you? For example, is there a piece of personal philosophy that best describes your sense of human relations? Or, is there a moment in history that seems to you to best capture the nature of society? How might (or have) these things influenced your creative writing?

If you were asked to name one main thing you were 'aiming for' in doing some creative writing, what would it be? Is there more than one – a set of aims, perhaps, some more important to you than others? If that is the case, is it possible to prioritise these aims in any way – for example, in how you spend your time, in what you read, in the ways you combine leisure time and work time?

3
Passions for Creative Writing

I must admit to being personally interested in the idea, often mentioned to those starting writing creatively, that the act of creative writing comes with a particular kind, or strength, of passion for the labour of doing it. Sometimes it's even called an 'obsession'. Maybe it's the same with all artists. Maybe it's not unique to the Arts. Do you think there is anything in this 'passion' or 'obsession' notion, at all?

What drives any of us to want to write creatively? Not everyone does it, so is there something recognisable about those of us who do? Is there something different about doing it only now and then, just doing it once or twice, or doing it all your life? Could the words 'passion' or 'obsession' be applied to a long-term interest in creative writing?

I recall here some of Frank Conroy's comments in his introduction to *The Eleventh Draft: Craft and the Writing Life from the Iowa Writers' Workshop*. Conroy, as many will know, was the 5th Director of the famed Iowa Writers Workshop, an accomplished writer, and sometime director of the literature programme at the National Endowment for the Arts. His comments on creative writing go like this:

> It's a hard life because one is dependent on forces that are not fully understood and usually impossible to control. It's scary, because most writers in the midst of making a novel or a short story don't really know if their work is bad or good. Most

of them operate on faith. Many of them, having completed a strong piece of work, are not confident they can ever do it again. These fears, and others, are in fact commonplace, and one of the immediate benefits of joining a community of writers is precisely that discovery.[1]

Without being overly trite, ask yourself: does this sound like a great deal of fun?! Something that is 'impossible to control', 'scary' and initiates 'fears' – this doesn't immediately conjure up the idea of a thing that is going to be attractive to anyone at all, and definitely not something with which we might choose to engage long-term. Conroy goes on to say that 'a certain amount of uncomfortableness simply comes with the territory'. In which case, it might be worth wondering why you would want to do this kind of thing – voluntarily!

Psychologist Daniel Nettle, in a chapter entitled 'The Evolution of Creative Writing' suggests that 'an obvious explanation of why people write creatively is that they can achieve prestige and good regard by doing so.'[2] Perhaps ask yourself, is this *your* reason for writing creatively? Do we sense this widely when talking to creative writers about their creative writing? If so, is this specific to creative writing, or even specific to the arts generally? Is it, say, the same reason people get involved in film-making? Renowned film director, writer and producer Ingmar Bergman, writing in the mid-twentieth century, remarked:

> I feel an irrepressible need to express in film that which, completely subjectively, is part of my consciousness. In this case I have therefore no other goal but *myself*, my daily bread, the amusement and respect of the public, a sort of truth that I find to be right at that particular moment.[3]

While it sounds like being held in 'good regard' takes some part in the way Bergman is thinking, it is not the end point for his emotional or intellectual engagement with film-making and it certainly isn't the only thing going on for him. Equally, the reference to that 'irrepressible' need seems to point to something over which he has little control. In other words, by 'need' he seems to suggest that it is a powerful determinant not merely a casual choice, and by 'irrepressible' he also seems to suggest that restraining himself from expressing himself in film would be either very difficult or entirely impossible. Why?

No one would surely suggest that it is *only* ever possible to be a creative writer if you have a narrow range of personality traits suitable for being one, or if you have strength of a certain kind that can get you through what Frank Conroy refers to as the 'uncomfortableness'. And yet, it would be difficult not to conclude that there is something going on, some urge or inclination, attitude or dispositional trait. Odysseus Elytis, 1979 Nobel Prize Laureate, Greek poet, translator and essayist, says 'after poetry, painting was my greatest passion'.[4] Note, these are his *passions*, not his pastimes, not his occupations, not his vices and not his amusements. I doubt the word passion is chosen here without some element of prior thought. On the other hand, Dorothea Brande in *Becoming a Writer*, a book that has often appeared on the reading list of creative writing courses, suggests that:

> [B]ecoming a writer is mainly a matter of cultivating a writer's temperament. Now the very word 'temperament' is justly suspect among well-balanced persons, so I hasten to say that it is not part of the program to inculcate a wild-eyed bohemianism, or to set up moods and caprices as necessary accompaniments of the author's life. On the contrary; the moods and tempers, when they actually exist, are the systems of the artist's personality gone wrong – running off into waste effort and emotional exhaustion.[5]

Though somewhat essentialist in outlook, Brande's aims in *Becoming a Writer* are laudable and the book is rightly well-loved; but in the many decades since her book's first publication much additional work has been undertaken on creativity, on the nature of the arts, and on human cognition, dispositions and personalities. In short, the notion of there being a singular 'artist's personality' is very hard to swallow, and the effect of the word 'temperament' and the idea of 'cultivating' one that is appropriate for a writer is to limit how we might approach the incredible variety of individuals who engage in creative writing. While we can find similarities and discover commonalities in outlook and approach we surely can't dismiss the power of human free will or the ability of one or other of us to approach creative writing in our personal way.

In asking Question 3 – *Do you think there is anything in this 'passion' or 'obsession' notion, at all?* – I admit, with hindsight, to contemplating that I had made a mistake. I felt I was using the word 'obsession' simply to suggest something that goes beyond the rational, beyond the mere logical. I was thinking of something along the lines of Bergman's 'irrepressible need'. My intention was to try and discover if the creative writers I was contacting felt something that was not easily nailed down in terms of rational choice. An emotional context, then, or a mental state not solely determined by conscious thought, a strong feeling.

But the word 'obsession' can suggest – and its complete definition indeed does suggest this – some kind of unreasonable intensity, even a kind of affliction. That was not what I had meant to suggest. Things that we are passionate about can produce actions and thoughts that go beyond the purely rational. But the intention of using the word 'obsession' was not primarily to suggest a burden, even if the creative writing work required to accomplish what we seek to accomplish is sometimes intense. Perhaps it would have been better to have stuck with the word 'passion'! The creative writers, despite my later misgivings, usefully explored both terms.

* * *

Iain Banks

Not for me. I love writing and I miss it if I don't write something sizable for a couple of years, but it's not obsession.

Charles Baxter

Most writers have a mild form of obsessive-compulsive disorder. They have to. Every detail has to be right, or the book as a whole is no good. If the details don't match up, readers will notice. My son is a bridge engineer and bridge designer; he's obsessive too, and he has to be, because a bridge that hasn't been designed properly, with obsessive attention to detail, is going to fall down.

Andy Brown

Absolutely! But then I'm extraordinarily lucky, I've always been surrounded by enthusiastic and talented people: writers, musicians, directors, producers, artists, sculptors, photographers, and so on. On the other hand, I've also been surrounded by people who aren't involved in the Arts at all, but who are, nonetheless, passionate about what they do: scientists, ecologists, gardeners, cooks, postmen, mothers, and fathers. I've always loved enthusiasts. I seek them out. In my lucky circle of experience, energy has generated more energy: a little of it rubs off on me from others, and bang! Nuclear fission. And energy, passion, and bloody-mindedness are exactly what you need to write, because it's hard work. It's not digging coal, sure, but it's damned hard work: it's lonely, isolating, and emotionally and intellectually exhausting. What we often don't understand when we start out writing is that writing is re-writing is re-writing is re-writing ... Only an obsessive body and mind will get you through that; only someone with an enduring passion for words and the world will honour that contract. This obsession is both its own yawning chasm and its own sublime reward. If you're ready for that, then there is nothing more rewarding than hearing a reader tell you that they too are passionate about something you have written; that something you have written has changed them. It's that two-way communication that this obsessive business of writing and reading is about.

Maggie Butt

Yes, all my life I have been a ravenous reader and an obsessive scribbler. I kept a daily diary from the age of 11 to 21, and at various high and low periods since (definitely not for public consumption!) I had written several bookfuls of poetry, plentiful short stories and my first (unpublished) novel, by the time I was 21. It's an urge, a need, which wells up; words form in the mind and have to be written down – as essential as breathing.

Jack Epps Jr.

If you are not obsessed – driven – then you probably won't have much success in the entertainment field. When I was getting started writing, getting a movie made was my entire life. It was a twenty-four-hour a day job. I never stopped thinking about the script I was working on – always trying to find a better way to tell the story. You have to be selfish and the career comes first. End of story. Anything less and you should look for something else to do. Totally devoted or nothing.

At this point in my writing, I've learned how to get to the story and the characters quicker. I'm experienced enough that I am disciplined enough to focus and make better use of my time. I have a family and enjoy my time with them very much, but I waited to have a family until I was launched with a solid career. Then I could do it more on my own terms.

Writing is hard – it never gets easier – not if you have high standards. It does get quicker, so you have to want it – have that desire that will push you through the loneliness and isolation. I think that probably the hardest part of being a writer is feeling alone. That's one of the reasons I worked in a partnership. I really enjoy the social aspect of making a film. I do enjoy working with directors. I like being part of a team. We are all pulling for the same thing – make the best film possible.

Nadine Gordimer

'Obsession' suggests an abnormality. Writing, painting is the reason-to-be for those respectful of being somehow born with the talent.

Kate Grenville

No one is waiting with bated breath for you to write another paragraph. Newspapers never headline writers' block the way they do groin strains. The world doesn't care whether your book gets written or not. So you do have to be driven by something that comes from within.

I think the obsessive quality is the fascination that goes with any rich kind of problem-solving. A novel is a gigantic set of interlocking problems to solve – a giant Sudoku or set of dove-tail joints. As a species we do seem hard-wired to enjoy problem-solving, and writing is just one way of entering that mix of pleasure and frustration.

Writing a novel is a gigantic task – it takes me around 3 or 4 years and a couple of dozen drafts – only some deep interior drive can get you through that.

Nessa O'Mahony

I've tended to see it more as an addiction, rather than a passion, because the need to write, and the unpleasant symptoms one experiences when one isn't writing for any period of time, seems closer to over-reliance on certain stimulants than to an emotional attachment (or over-attachment) which passion or obsession might suggest. When I started writing creatively, rather than technically as a journalist or editor as I had been doing for a number of years, I found a way to use words in a personal way, to deal with personal concerns. That sounds very subjective, but it was such a huge relief to be able to chart my own world after all that verbiage I'd produced on behalf of other people about subjects that I was only remotely interested in. So I quickly became addicted during those brief creative holidays I had from the day job and, like coffee, I still haven't been able to quit.

Ruth Padel

No idea. Just can't imagine going through life without writing.

Robert Pinsky

Some people keep working at a sport, or a kind of music, or some craft of wood or metal. Gardening. Building a boat in the basement or garage, or at ambitious projects in knitting or sewing. We are a making animal, and devotion to some particular form of making is not unusual among us. In certain forms, to a certain degree, the term 'art' becomes appropriate.

I had a false start in one art, but in retrospect I feel I was always destined for another.

Philip Pullman

The labour is mostly repetitive and dismal toil. I have no appetite for it. I take it up with reluctance and put it down with relief. Every time I write a sentence, I intend it to be the last time I look at it. Of course, it never is; but I just want to get it behind me. However, I do agree that there may be if not a passion then a sort of affinity for the *material*, as a cabinet-maker just loves touching wood and knows how to get the best out of it. I have that affinity with language. I am at home with it, I can see without effort if and where and why it's going wrong, I know how to bargain with it so as to get it to conform a little more exactly to what I think I want to say, and so on. Some people have that sense with music. I imagine they write sonatas and symphonies.

Tom Shapcott

You have to have great persistence. That, presumably, is another word for 'obsession'. Yes, without that essential drive, that need not only to 'get it down' but also to do it the best way you can, well, you remain essentially a dilettante. When I was 15 I won a prize in the local eisteddfod (Ipswich had a large Welsh mining population) but the girl who won the 'open' section, who was a year older, wrote a much finer poem. She did not keep up her writing; I did.

William Tremblay

Is writing an obsession?

Jack Kerouac has his narrator Sal Paradise say in *On the Road* that 'you have to stick to it with the devotion of a benny addict.' I've already said that for me it is a physiological need. I might as well add, in the antithetical spirit of Whitman, that it is equally an aversion. There are times when I would rather cut off my hand than pick up a pen. This may not sound all that encouraging, but it is true. You have to have as much courage and patience as inspiration in the act of writing. Maybe that's why so many writers have said that writing is about time.

Xu Xi

I am a complete believer in passion bordering on obsession for anyone who wishes to excel (not just be competent) in a given industry. No it's not unique to the arts. Creative writing students who complain about having to submit too many pages yet want to be a published novelist really get a tongue lashing from me; ditto undergrads who want to write poetry (or whatever genre) and then simply cannot name a single poet they have read or like (which is why I do NOT teach undergrads!). Passion allows you to accept rejection and move on, to acknowledge and confront your weaknesses in the given industry and try to improve because you so desperately want to excel in it. Do you know the Peter Principle, oft cited in business? That we all rise to our levels of incompetence (or words to that effect)? The other thing about passion for a writer is that you still keep trying in the face of your own incompetence, because you want it badly enough (whatever 'it' might be – finishing a book, publication, writing a poetry cycle of sonnets, etc.) The doing of it is where most of the passion really goes – to succeed is just icing.

*   *   *

Toil, labour, hard work – the problem we often face in creative writing is just how distinctive some things might be to it, and how common other things might be, even if we sometimes *claim* them as unique to creative writing. Is creative writing any harder than any other kind of human activity – sometimes, all the time, by its very nature, or any other fashion? Some finished works of creative writing – the novel would be a good example – come with a certain general suggestion of a work ethic. The novel, in this sense, is often seen to be a long haul, a matter of human endurance as well as creative inspiration. A poem, however, might be something created in a moment.

I'm generalising here about our shared impressions of these things. Nevertheless, some truth exists in such a generalisation. That is, that we tend to locate certain dispositional ideals in creative writing and certain traits in those who undertake creative writing. Maybe, however, this is not as straightforward as it might appear. Xu Xi believes in a 'passion bordering on obsession for anyone who wishes to excel (not just be competent) in a given industry', while Ruth Padel says she 'just can't imagine going through life without writing'. Andy Brown feels that 'this obsession is both its own yawning chasm and its own sublime reward', while Kate Grenville says that she feels 'the obsessive quality is the fascination that goes with any rich kind of problem-solving'. An interesting mix of responses!

Almost certainly someone exclaiming 'Wow, really, you wrote a novel?!' would also be declaring something to do with the effort, and something to do with our cultural impressions of the novel form. If you replied, 'Oh sure, I wrote it last week, just when I stopped work to have a quick coffee' it wouldn't only be amazement that you'd find, there would most likely also be elements of what might best be called disappointment, or scepticism, or even envy and concern. After all, you couldn't *possibly* have written a good novel in your spare time, over a short period, without some spookily inhuman input.

I'm exaggerating, but the point is that each public document in creative writing, each distributed example of creative writing, carries with it some general impression about what was involved in its composition (something here of Jack Epps Jr.'s: 'It was a twenty four hour a day job. I never stopped thinking about the script I was working on – always trying to find a better way to tell the story'). You might ask the question of someone: 'Which involves a greater effort, writing a collection of short stories or completing a screenplay?' Or, 'Which is more emotionally engaging, the writing of a piece of journalism or the writing of a poem?' In essence, these are 'how long is a piece of string' questions, but the answers you receive might be revealing – revealing for you too, that is, about how you view the relationship between effort and passion.

When we are exploring what drives us to write creatively, what is *actually* involved in doing it, we do find evidence of persistence, devotion and passion. To suggest such human responses are only associated with creative writing wouldn't make a great deal of sense. However, there are two key ways of approaching what might be particular about creative writing in this regard.

Firstly, particular end results of creative writing symbolise certain things about the act of creative writing, culturally (Kate Grenville's 'writing a novel is a gigantic task' fits well here). So, the novel tends to symbolise the effort involved in creative writing. The poem symbolises the inspired, or the momentary capturing of brilliance. The play symbolises the collaborative, even if the piece is composed by the person who then performs it and involves no other persons in its making. Again these are *considerable* generalisations, but the reference point in any of these assumptions is the finished artefacts, the completed works. The truth of how these works are made might not always correspond well to the assumptions, but the importance of these assumptions to how these works are understood shouldn't be underestimated.

Secondly, though, there is the association of our creative writing with something that cannot be explained solely in terms of consciousness or logic. Something that is related to words and their use; but, that goes beyond simple communication and appears to be akin to the kinds of metaphysical engagements we see from other artists. That something is incredibly individual: it is based in almost entirely in the individual self.

Exercise

What are your expectations when undertaking a piece of creative writing? That is, if you were writing a novel what would your expectations be about the way you would undertake it? Would the writing happen at certain times of the day, in a certain place, engaging in the work in a particular fashion? Is it possible for you to write down some narrative comparisons between writing one work, or work in one genre, and work in another? Tell the comparative story of the making of these works (suggested word length for this exercise: 1000–1500 words)

Reflection

Because the term might indeed be the wrong term, let's explore it! That is, do you think there is anything *obsessive* about doing creative writing? If so, in what sense, and to what result?

If creative writers have particular strengths what, for you, would seem the most important ones? Is it as straightforward as saying 'creative writers need to be good at using words'? Are there things associated with creative writing that are not primarily skills-based? For example, do creative writers need to approach the world in any particular way?

4
That Word 'Creative'

A tough one, this one, but I've wondered nevertheless. The key word that separates creative writing from other forms of writing is that slippery word 'creative'. Do you think much about it? Or about creativity, generally? Do you feel it joins you to other artists in any way? Or, indeed, does it separate you at all from those not involved in 'creative' activities? This is probably a question about 'creating' as an activity; though it's perhaps a badly phrased question!

The word 'creative', along with our many concepts and ideas that relate to it, initiates more questions than it answers. Frankly, it is both the best of descriptions and the worst of descriptions for anything we might do. This isn't because 'creative' is not *trying* to say something; and not because the majority of things it is trying to say would be considered negative, or detrimental, to us personally or to humankind generally. However, the remarkable nature of the 'creative' is both a strength and a weakness in coming to understand what it is that we are endeavouring to describe by using the term in the first place.

Rob Pope begins his discussion 'Why Creativity Now?' in his book *Creativity: Theory, History, Practice*, by commenting:

> Creativity is of immediate interest to just about everyone. Am I creative? How creative am I? Can I become more creative? But no one can think or talk about it for long without getting into highly involved issues: about whether only certain special

people are creative or everyone is potentially creative in some way; and whether some activities – or cultures or periods – are more creative than others.[1]

Indeed. And by choosing to call something 'creative' writing we don't necessarily clarify what it is – though we are certainly pointing towards something. Earlier, I explored the idea of creative writing being graspable by thinking of it as something to do with a particular method of using words. That can be a way for us to define when we personally feel we began (or begin) creative writing; and to be reasonably confident about what we consider we're doing when we're undertaking some creative writing. However, even this is not entirely clear cut. This is not least because we're then in the unenviable position of having to decide when it is that our writing becomes *more creative* and when it becomes *less creative*. Perhaps it becomes so 'not creative' that it is no longer creative writing at all!

The danger here is that the search for a definition actually produces pedantry rather than real, usable knowledge. Knowledge you can use as a creative writer. Knowledge that others, who are not creative writers, can use to at least have some concept of that with which you are engaged. So, there may be some practical as well as theoretical value in exploring these ideas, but we're not getting an awful lot closer to clarity about what the 'creative' entails.

In this way, the nature of the creative remains enigmatic, and therefore so does the nature of 'creative' writing. In effect, saying something is creative writing is a determination of intention as well as an approach, an outlook as well as an art form, an action as well as an end result. But is it all these things because of its relationships with creativity? Opening his discussion of creativity, Mihaly Csikszentmihalyi suggests:

The answer is obvious: Creativity is some sort of mental activity, an insight that occurs inside the heads of some special people. But this sort of assumption is misleading. If by creativity we mean an action that is new and valuable, then we cannot simply accept a person's own account as the criterion for its existence. There is no way to know whether a thought is new except with reference to some standards, and there is no way to know whether it is valuable until it passes social evaluation. Therefore creativity does not happen inside people's heads, but in the interaction between a person's thoughts and a sociocultural context.[2]

The suggestion here has some validity: socio-cultural context undoubtedly impacts us all, and therefore creativity could be said to reside beyond us personally. But does an individual creative writer's thoughts about creativity determine their approach to creative writing? Likewise, if you are writing creatively are you aware that you are behaving in particular ways, thinking in particular ways, approaching the world in particular ways, and responding to the imaginative in particular ways? If so then creativity, in a very important and real sense, *does* happen inside a person's head and Csikszentmihaly is wrong. In addition, how, when and why it happens does indeed determine both the actions you undertake and the end result of those actions.

We individuals are not merely a collection of social and cultural determinants, the result of structures and systems and societal activities beyond ourselves. Not solely, not only. This is never more obvious than when we begin to think about the creative. The creative returns us to ourselves, as well as referring to the society around us. Whether it absolutely depends on what Csikszentmihaly calls 'sociocultural context' likewise depends on how we view the strength of our individual human dispositions, our individual psychology, individual personalities, including our own personality – to a large extent our beliefs about the relationship between our nature and our nurture.

Attempting to define creativity, while difficult, asks us to consider what it is that makes the human activity of creative writing distinctive. Relatively simple references to types of word use and to the end results (novels, poems, scripts) give us a form of general definition, an easy point of reference. But one of the great strengths of the creative is its recognition of individuality and free choice, as well as its grounding in our wider societies and cultures. It's not that creativity defies definition but it is that its definitions don't help us as much as *descriptions of the actual doing*.

There is one final thing, which probably does not actually need saying: creativity is right at the core of so much human action.

While it might remain one of our most enigmatic subjects, even possibly a subject that will *always* generate more questions than it will ever answer, it would be sorely missed if somehow it no longer happened! As well as constituting the primary mode of the arts, the creative is also a collection of wider human actions and traits, assisting our survival and enhancing our enjoyment of life. The creative plays a role in our sense of ourselves, as well as contributing to our sense of the world.

* * *

Iain Banks

I have thought and do think about it a fair bit because it's the one question that I expected to get asked that I do get asked all the time: Where do you get your ideas from? The answer is the same place as everybody else. Everybody has ideas, even if they're only in the shape of sexual fantasies or what they'd do if they won the lottery. Writers and other creative people just do this more intensely and self-consciously, and we exploit it. There's a passage in my book *Raw Spirit* – nominally about whisky – that goes into more detail regarding this. I think this predisposition – this attitude/way of looking at the world – does link almost all artists and creative people. As usual in such matters, it's partly something you're born with and something you can choose to develop as a skill.

Charles Baxter

The composer Ned Rorem once said that true artists as adults don't talk abstractly about creativity. They talk about money, commissions, and the like. I once thought about creativity but now think in extremely practical terms about how to do something I want to do in a novel or a story. I think about the craft, the practicalities.

Andy Brown

To be honest, no, I don't think much about it at all. I'm not very interested in theories of creativity; I just know that I recognise and love creativity in others and in myself. What joins me to others, I hope, is alert, open-minded, enthusiastic *being*, rather than 'creativity' in any abstract sense. I know plenty of very creative people who aren't involved in the Arts, as I noted above. What we share has something to do with our human *being*; our sense of connectedness; our sense of being in the world. I don't feel separate from others because I'm 'creative' and they're not; I don't see it like that at all. Science is supposedly not 'creative', but I've never found it to be 'uncreative'. In fact, quite the opposite. Scientific observation, poetic observation, spiritual observations; they're all part and parcel of the same human thing – profound expression in the face of wonders, however big or small those wonders may be.

On the other hand, I certainly do share a great deal of 'creativity' with people who are in the Arts. All the music I have ever done, for example, has been entirely collaborative, as have been some of my poetry projects and publications. And I've spent my life surrounded by writers, musicians and artists. Maybe 'creative' people just give off some kind of invisible glow, whether they're involved in the Arts or not, and it's that glow that I look for; it's that glow that both distinguishes and nourishes.

Maggie Butt

I think all forms of creativity feed one another and are connected to one another, so that if I draw (badly) or take photographs, or visit galleries, or listen to music, or go to the ballet, there's something I recognize in all those activities, and in others who do them.

I resisted the American academic terminology of 'creative writing' for a long time, believing it was a tautology, because all writing is 'creative'. However, I finally came to accept that if something is widely identified by a certain name, then it is sensible to use that name myself.

However, I do accept that writing as a journalist, or writing a letter or a diary, is a different sort of act from writing a poem or a story. Perhaps it's like natural birth and adoption. With poetry and stories you have to conceive the idea, and you have that little tingle which says 'here one comes', (and sometimes – let's be honest – great pleasure in the idea.) With journalism, diaries, letters, the idea is usually there already. You obviously have to work on it, bring it up, so to speak, and it's still your child, which you have formed, but there is an essential conceptual and imaginative difference. Perhaps even a 'creative' difference?

Jack Epps Jr.

To me writing is focused day dreaming. Clear and simple. I have an idea and let my mind wander. I try not to reign it in. Let it go and see where it ends up. Usually I end up with images. Moments of a scene and then I try and put context and a bit of structure to the idea. I'm not thinking about being creative. I'm just letting go. I've often said that high school was great training for being a writer. I was bored to tears and spent most of my time day dreaming out the window. When it came time to focus those day dreams as a screenwriter, it was second nature. I have easy access to my imagination.

Also, movies are a puzzle. I like putting together bits and pieces, and trying to structure them. Find the spine – the line of the movie. Once you find the line – you know what it's about, you can be playful with the idea. Build off the line.

I think creativity comes from letting go and not thinking. Analytical is counterproductive. Everything dies by dissection. Learn, explore, analyze, and then forget it. Young writers should rely upon their instincts. You can build instincts by watching the right movies, reading a ton of screenplays, but eventually you have to believe in your instincts and trust them. It's not as easy as it sounds. It takes a lot of practice.

Nadine Gordimer

'Creative' is a one-fits-all used for advertising copy etc. Writers don't think about it. They know the mysteries of the work they do.

Kate Grenville

I think 'creativity' is just another way of thinking about problem-solving – I don't think it's a special magic quality that only certain blessed people possess. It's not a matter of genre or form, for me, but the willingness to engage the imagination and think in new ways, make new connections between things. That means 'non-fiction' can be just as 'creative' as a poem.

Problem-solving in any context is about the willingness to take a risk. Creativity is the willingness to get it wrong a dozen times before you get it right. It's about not playing safe and certainly not playing to what you think the market or the audience will want. It's about recognising 'failure' as part of a process rather than an end point. Scientists understand this: they know a 'failed' experiment can actually tell you much more than a 'successful' one. Or, as the engineer Henri Petroski says, you learn much more when a bridge falls down than when it stays up.

Nessa O'Mahony

I think you can use the word creative as narrowly or as loosely as you like. People are always finding 'creative' solutions to problems, although maybe they are just clever rather than creative. I'll refer back to my answer to your previous question. For me, creative writing was, at the beginning, a way of exploring subjective experience and that differentiated it from other types of writing I was doing at the time. Since then, it has broadened out considerably, but it still involves a use of the imagination, liminal and subliminal, that I don't find much use for elsewhere. So I do think there's a common bond between all people who use their imaginations in similar ways, regardless of the art-form.

Ruth Padel

I think good science needs as much imagination and 'creativity' as writing. That word 'creative' should be dropped from the language.

Robert Pinsky

In a sense 'creating' is easy, cheap, available: the mind pours out little fantasies and systems in a perpetual messy gush. The art is in what one manages to do with all of that fantasy or babble: choosing, refining, setting it to music, or mining it, or navigating it. Sometimes just slowing it down seems the great goal or gift.

As I've said, I don't think the artist is an entirely special case: everyone tries to make their conversation effective or amusing; in that sense, everyone composes or 'writes' all day long. Some use slang or professional jargon inventively and originally, some use it in a tedious, hackneyed way; that is like art.

When a teenager chooses a pattern or rhythm of 'like's, or when anyone makes a pattern or rhythm of obscenities – that's a bit like 'writing.'

Philip Pullman

I don't think about it at all. Not for a moment. It really isn't of the slightest interest, and I'm not avoiding the question for fear of giving away any secrets, or for any other reason. I just don't think about it. Nor do I think about other artists. What's more, talk or writing about 'creativity' seems rather like talk or writing about 'spirituality' – I just avoid getting involved in that sort of conversation, because I can't get any sense of what it means. People seem to use the words in ways that make sense to them, but to me it looks like a game whose rules I don't understand played with counters that have no value.

Tom Shapcott

I don't think the word 'creative' is much help. We are all creative in some sense. Certainly in teaching, I try to get students to tap into their own wellspring of feeling/response. Those with greater life experience usually find this easier, of course. But even so we are more than simply learning or listening machines. If what emerges is 'creativity' so be it; but it is also the personal in the manifold.

William Tremblay

What is 'creative' in creative writing?

I start from Blake on that one. Blake says, and I'm paraphrasing, that if all you want to do is measure the dimensions of your prison then factual representation is all that you need. But if you want to get out of your prison you need an imagination. That means representing what you dream and hope for rather than what you've got.

The first creative act of a creative person is to create the persona who is capable of creating, has attributes of active receptivity.

Also the 'creation' takes place within the audience, whether that audience is you or not. Think of it in terms of montage: Sergei

Eisenstein juxtaposes an image of Czarist soldiers firing rifles at the top of the Odessa steps with an image of a dowager's spectacles shattered and bloody. What he has 'created' is the invitation to an inference, i.e. one of the bullets has entered her brain through her eye. And, yes, she falls to the cobblestone harbour pavement dead. So, paradoxically, he has created by erasing the middle term.

Willa Cather has a statement about that subject. To paraphrase, she says that creation happens when a word which has scrupulously not been mentioned occurs in the mind of the reader.

Xu Xi

Yes, I do think it separates me from those not in the creative arts, and yes, I do feel a bond with other serious artists that I might not when I meet a pilot or beautician. Having said that, I don't really think a whole lot about creativity generally because it is by now just a given in my life. When I didn't know a lot of writers and artists, I pondered the question more, because I wondered about identity that was tied to creativity. These days, I sometimes prefer to hang with pilots or beauticians and let the writers and artists wallow in their own angst – I mean I love to party with writers and painters especially, but my artist friends can sometimes strain the friendship with their creative angst and there are days I want nothing to do with the creative crowd. But this generally passes because my life tends to take me to that world regularly anyway.

* * *

Think about creativity or not think about creativity? Creative writers don't necessarily push themselves to think about creativity simply because we widely use the term 'creative writing' to define what we are doing. For some, thinking about creativity is a distraction. For others, some ideas about the creative might contribute to ideals that relate to their involvement in creative writing. If there is a majority view in the answers to the question here then it probably is on the side of not thinking about 'that slippery word 'creative''. However, the jury is still out!

Iain Banks mentions: 'I have thought and do think about it a fair bit' and Xu Xi says in her response that 'yes, I do think it separates me from those not in the creative arts'. Tom Shapcott finds: 'I don't think the word 'creative' is much help' and Philip Pullman says 'I don't think about it at all. Not for a moment'. Maggie Butt says 'I think all forms of creativity feed one another and are connected to one another', but Kate Grenville approaches the question by noting that 'I think "creativity" is just another way of thinking about problem-solving – I don't think it's a special magic quality that only certain blessed people possess.' Needless to say these, and the other responses here, provide a wonderful cross-section of thoughts that lead us back to the question of whether a definition of creativity is much use to creative writers at all and perhaps lead even to Nadine Gordimer's comment that writers 'know the mysteries of the work they do'.

Predictably, even if definitions are useful, circumscribed definitions of creativity are seen by these writers to be of little or no assistance. Alternatively, ideas about the creative that explore origins of ideas, or suggest ways of thinking, are not seen to be entirely without merit, and might even have some very positive value in framing the ways in which creative writers approach the actions of writing, or even their ways of thinking.

How about that word 'thinking'? It was an assumption I made earlier that creative action and thinking have a relationship. It is more accurate to say that too narrow a concept of 'thinking' fails to really approach creativity, and that any suggestion of thinking as primarily connected with rationality or intellectual activity misses a great deal of what the creative actually entails.

As can be seen from the responses of the creative writers here, creative writing is often *very* personal action and thinking. What is meant by thinking in this instance might not occur for us purely as rational thought. The emotive and the sensory play considerable roles in our creative writing. In other words, your emotions and your senses are equally engaged when you are writing creatively, and their relationship with the creative is not something that can be reduced to an intellectualised rationality. Creative writing is not based solely on reason.

Questions arise also about our imaginations and explorations they undertake of what is *not* in right front of us. Mental images, representing our imaginative speculations, or scenarios based on a combination of what we see or what we know and what we *project*. When we say 'creative' we sometimes mean 'imaginative'. These are not the same thing. The creative designates a new thing, something made; whereas the imaginative can just as easily designate the image of something not in front of us, but that is not a new thing. If the creative refers to the new and the imaginative is more specifically related to the projection of mental images of something then in this sense creative writing can indeed be *both* creative and imaginative.

Considering all this might not necessarily provide practical clues to problems of composition in creative writing. It might not solve a stylistic question for you or help you to structure a story or poem. But it does help put in context the interactions between our minds and our bodies that are taking place when we are engaged in creative writing. It alerts us to remarkable and exciting dimensions of what we're attempting.

Reflection

If there is a difference between the imaginative and the creative, can you determine those things you do that you'd define as 'imaginative' and those you'd define as 'creative'? Does it matter? If so, why? If not, why do you think we often use these two words in similar ways?

Exercise

It is sometimes difficult to define where creative writing begins and other kinds of writing end. Try writing a short passage (suggested word length for this exercise: 100–300 words) you would define as 'not creative writing'. And then try dealing with the same material in a form you would say 'is creative writing'? How do you make the distinction between these two activities?

Reflection

Human creativity is all around us, and we also see the word 'creative' used for such a wide variety of activities, from those in the arts to those in business, the sciences, in education. A trip to an art gallery or a concert, watching a film, playing an online game or observing the structure and design of buildings around us brings us into contact with creativity in some of the other arts. If as a creative writer you find an affinity emerging from these other arts can you briefly describe it? If you don't find an affinity, is there anything else you do feel best relates to your own sense, and practice, of creating?

5
The Idea of Drafting

Probably a good bridge to something less esoteric is a question about drafting. Do you feel you have a fairly good sense, these days, about how you write? I don't mean, that you can predict exactly how things might run. But, do you at least feel you're ready for things that might occur along the way? If so, is there anything particular that you know will probably happen (for example: you know you might visit 'structure' a fair bit; or, you know that you'll probably need to do additional research of some kind after the first draft – anything like that)?

Often in discussing creative writing we return to some basics of how we make things in the world. In the case of undertaking what might be called the 'work at hand' we are reminded that so very frequently a work of art does not emerge *exactly* as we might like it to be, and we need to produce several 'drafts' of a work before we're satisfied with it enough to allow it to be considered 'done'.

As we've seen, definitions sometimes do overburden discussions and here is another good example of that overburdening! What is a draft in creative writing terms, and what isn't a draft? When is a piece of your creative writing done, and when isn't it done? Can we come up with any sense in which a piece of your creative writing takes a linear journey from the origination of an idea or emotion, perhaps, to your completed work, a play, a poem, a novel?

As you'll see in Chapter 12, creative writing is frequently anything *but* a linear journey. You could start writing a story and stop writing it several times before it is finished. You could write that story over a short period of time or, stopping and starting, it might take you years to complete. Other pieces of writing could emerge in the meantime. You might have an idea for a poem, write the whole thing in an hour, and then decide that this poem is not very good and leave it sitting for some years. Noticing the poem in a pile of scrap paper, you could be struck by a phrase, a word, and write a completely new poem, a very good poem, beginning with that found phrase. Is the earlier piece of work therefore a draft of the latter work, or is it something else? And what about the situation where you seem to complete something almost all in one go, no delays, no rethinking, finished? Do you then wonder if you should have gone through some additional process, if the absence of some preparatory, drafting work (at least in a physical, observable sense) means that this piece of creative writing could not *possibly* be done?

The word drafting suggests crafting, a bringing into being through a succession of our contributions, drawn from a level of knowledge that at least can attempt to make a piece of work better. Unquestionably, that idea of 'making better' defines what we mean by 'drafting'. It is often a kind of lament if a creative writer comments that 'my earlier draft was better'. What we all want to be able to say is that we began with something that was raw but had potential and we used our creative writing skills to make that something much better. We want to be able to say that the effort and the result somehow match each other. And we want to be able to believe that this comes about not only because of our ability to do something but also because of our ability to do it in an informed way.

Belief in our individual *understanding* lies behind drafting. How could it not? After all, what 'drafting' suggests is that you will have enough understanding of creative writing to be able to make decisions about what is good and what is not yet good in your own work. You will be able to determine if more work is needed. Even more importantly, your understanding will be matched by your *ability* to do that work in a way that ensures those improvements occur. No wonder there is a sense of disappointment when one of our later drafts doesn't match the qualities of an earlier draft. That suggests the understanding and/or ability was not there in the first place. Equally, even though drafting is conceptually about moving from a raw piece of writing to a refined piece of writing, from the not so good to very good, it's incredibly difficult to see any of this as a linear progression from a start to a finish.

This is because the making of a piece of creative writing requires varieties of aesthetic judgement. It involves a considerable number of individual and cultural encounters with subjects and themes. It naturally involves the use of written language and some sense of how that language conveys an emotional context; of how that written language can form the basis of an exchange between the writer and their audience. In all this, to suggest that in some staged, single direction we can move from a point of beginning to a point of ending is certainly counterintuitive, if not plainly ridiculous.

Add to this the ways in which your creative writer's mind processes immediate stimulus (for example, a sight or a sound), and the workings of your memory (memory tends to work in a connective, often non-chronological fashion). Add these things together, and the concept of a writing draft that is the product of taking one step simply after another becomes even more unlikely for any creative writer. It's worth considering, then, what ultimately does hold together the concept of drafting as 'making better'? Forms of belief, we might say.

The expression here is 'the *concept* of drafting', not because that is aiming to take us away from the *action* of drafting our work, but because we must have some concept of what we are doing, some thoughts about it, before, during and after doing it. After all, when do we know we are finished if we don't have a concept of what we've being doing? As with a great deal in arts practice, whatever knowledge we have is applied both to the idea of what needs doing and the decisions about when it is done.

In summary, drafting can often be non-linear, can involve considerable variations in time and effort (Your drafting timeframe might be completely different to another writer's drafting timeframe), and it often occurs according to the surrounding life of the creative writer. Drafting can be impacted upon by your memory as well as by your surrounding stimulus, and it can be approached with varying degrees of enthusiasm, belief and ability.

When asking the creative writers here about drafting the focus of my inquiry was on knowledge – what they individually might know that could make their understanding of their own drafting greater and their expectations more clear. Because drafting concerns work-at-hand the focus of this question was, indeed, on writing in motion, rather than on what appears at the end of that process.

*   *   *

Iain Banks

I have a very accurate idea how a book will run once I'm towards the end of the planning stage. I discovered that what works for me is to plan thoroughly before I start to write and then to stick to the plan when I do sit down to write (in the sense of the physical keyboard clattering that produces the text itself); otherwise I over-write, paint myself into corners, forget I'd killed off a character ten chapters ago ... that sort of thing. I've been writing this way for well over thirty years, so it's pretty much ingrained now.

Charles Baxter

Well, the American writer William Maxwell once said that everything he had learned was never of much use when he started a new book. He exaggerated, of course. You remember how to use commas and how to get characters through the door. But that's the elementary stuff. I never feel as if I know exactly how to do something the work might require beforehand; I have to learn how to do it by doing it. I don't want to know how I write – that is, I don't want to know too much about the process, although, as a critic, I suppose I have to know such matters. I just want to do it.

Andy Brown

For me, writing poems seems to happen in two main ways: I either write poems longhand in notebooks that come all in one go, as an expression of need, or experience, or as an immediate response to something I'm fascinated by and want to explore; or I work on longer-term pieces on the computer. The longhand, notebook poems, tend to come to me through immediate experiences, or chance finds, or linguistic things that catch my ear, and are more immediate and less mediated than the computer-written poems. The poems I write on computer tend towards greater formal and linguistic artifice – I often work on six or seven of them together at any one time, moving words and phrases around within and between poems, shaping the whole lot sculpturally, looking for shapes and patterns within the material that I've got. It's a very physical, tangible process: language is a plastic medium. Sequences can emerge at this point too. Both kinds of poem – longhand and computer – require different kinds of writing skills. I try to balance my dedication to both.

Once I've got a reasonable first draft, of either kind of poem, I get them typed up onto the computer and then go through a fairly typical kind of drafting/editing process: firstly I'll edit the poem for its SOUND; secondly for its IMAGERY; thirdly for other tonal effects of LANGUAGE, and lastly for its semantic MEANING. The sound is the most important one for me: poetry is a sound before it is anything else. It is then a sound fused with the *scope* of the imagination (by 'scope' I mean both the *range* of the imagination, and the *way* it sees), which is where image comes in. For me, the semantic meaning is the least interesting attribute of poetry: if I know what the poem is going to be *about* before I've really begun writing it, then I can't see much point in writing it; the pleasure for me lies in finding out what it all means through the process of writing and re-drafting. The poem itself is its own *aboutness*.

The other things that occupy a good deal of my thinking, of course, are questions of form and structure. I'm fascinated by formal concerns in poetry, itself perhaps too big a subject to tackle here. Save to say that some forms require a commitment on my part beforehand; that internal voice nagging at you which says 'This subject matter demands a sonnet, a prose poem, a sestina'. Other poems discover their form as they develop. Their form emerges. The number of times I've begun with a big block of raw material and ended up with another sonnet. I'm also fascinated in the power of poetic sequences, and so I begin to look for possible relationships between poems at an early stage. Sometimes you know you're writing a sequence at an early stage; other times you don't. It's a bit like going for a walk: you need to be open to the possibilities of the world around you; you need to be constantly aware; constantly on the look-out for what is hiding in-between the trees, under the stones, in amongst the grasses. For me, that's the great thrill of writing poems – language is such a thrilling partner to go for a walk with.

Maggie Butt

My writing process often goes like this:

1. A phrase or sentence coagulates in my mind – often as I'm going off to sleep, or walking, or driving, or in the shower. I write it down as soon as is safe /convenient. I keep a torch and notebook by the bed and a notebook in my handbag. Sometimes the act of pen to paper makes the initial words multiply of their own accord and I just keep writing. This sometimes feels like a direct download from the subconscious and can be very satisfying and sometimes utterly bizarre.
2. I transfer the fragment into my journal. Writing the initial ideas or phrases triggers new thoughts and I write these down, often in a sort of free prose. Sometimes a rhythm starts to appear in one line or two, which sets the form for the whole.
3. I type it into my lap-top, on the kitchen table, usually early in the morning, when the house is quiet and my brain is most active and alert. As I type, I begin to find a form. The word processor is a godsend, because you can move words and phrases around and try out a dozen different initial shapes for a poem. I keep going until I get to a sense of it being as far as I can go that day, until I feel I've used up my writing battery or I lose that sense of being 'in the zone.' I print this first draft.
4. After a few days I look at the printed version and make corrections, additions, alterations, perhaps do some research, perhaps read some poems in a certain form to see if that would be better.
5. Then back to the computer, to fiddle and sometimes completely re-write, as many times as it takes to feel I can't go any further.
6. Then I send the draft to one of a couple of trusted poet friends, or take it to my Stanza group. (See below.)
7. Multiple re-writes before sending it out into the world, to an editor. Though sometimes I do this too soon and re-work again later.

Making a poem for me begins with beachcombing – coming across a diamond in the rough, washed up by the tide, covered with barnacles – taking it home and trying to facet it, to bring out its brilliance. Occasionally I think I've done it justice, sometimes my hand slips and it's completely ruined, sometimes it turns out not to be a diamond at all, but a dull stone, and most often it feels passable, but as if something stunning has slipped away from me. Very, very rarely, I find it already polished and shining.

Jack Epps Jr.

Yes, I have an approach that I have used successfully for years. It's a way of getting to the heart of the project quicker and more accurately. I have better instincts. I've had movies produced and I've had the luxury of seeing what works and what doesn't work. Thankfully, more things work than don't work.

Finding the heart of the story is always the biggest challenge. What is this about? And who is it about? And why do we care? How does this story involve us? What makes this idea unique and worthy of getting a movie made? What are the stakes?

I know the right questions to ask and do not start until I have answered them. I also like to work out the story on scene cards before I begin to write the scenes. I'm not a believer of starting on page one and see where it turns out. To me that's like going on vacation and not knowing where you are heading. You're going to end up somewhere but it might not be where you want to go. And too many times it's a dead end. I just don't have that kind of time to waste. I only have so many screenplays in me and I want to make the best use of my time. I strongly believe a huge part of screenwriting is design.

I usually begin at the end and work my way back. If I know how the story will end up, then I can begin to figure out where I need to begin. Then it's a matter of linking the beginning and the ending. Again, easier said than done. The hard work is in the middle of a story. I sweat the middle and spend most of my time looking for ways to expand the story, relationships and characters.

Nadine Gordimer

My first drafts are done in my head. A short story occurs like an egg: complete, shell, white part, yolk where life is waiting. I know the beginning and the end, all that's in between. A novel is staked out between beginning and what's called the end: where I choose to put down, at some point, the lives invented.

Kate Grenville

The best thing I've learned from having been writing for so long is that it always feels like a failure. It always feels as if it will never work. It's always difficult. That means the gloom of failure is still keen, but I can now remind myself that all my books felt that way until they were finished.

I know I need to do many drafts. I can only write if I can tell myself 'never mind how bad it is, you can fix it up later'.

I know I can't write a book or a scene because I 'should'. No matter how good an idea seems in the abstract, if it doesn't excite me in the actual writing, there's no point flogging it along – just cut your losses and find that energy somewhere else.

I've learned not to show writing to anyone too soon – to live with a shapeless thing and just keep prodding and adding and re-arranging and exploring. Eventually it more or less lets you know what kind of a thing it might be. No one else can help you in that time.

Later on, though, the value of a good editor is huge. I don't mean someone who fixes your commas or makes small-scale tinkerings. I mean someone who reads the whole thing, goes away and thinks about it and engages their own imaginations so they can begin to sense what the book could be. Such people are rare, and publishers who will allow them that time even rarer, but it's the difference between an adequate book and a book that's as good as it can be.

Nessa O'Mahony

As a child of the computer era, I've always drafted on screen and thus edited as I go along. I've occasionally made efforts to write first drafts of poems longhand, in the belief that I would interrupt the flow of inspiration less this way, but I tend to get irritated by the lack of scope for editing! There's lots of wisdom around writing poems and then leaving them for a long time to bake; I wish I had the patience for that.

Ruth Padel

I do everything instinctively, so I can't really answer that, but of course structure is everything, all the time, at every stage. At the outset, though, the first 'charge' comes, and that is what will dictate the form, if you listen to what it is saying.

Robert Pinsky

In some ways it has become more difficult and bewildering than ever. I've always worked partly by resisting or upsetting or re-interpreting expectation. One of the people I must resist or thwart is Robert Pinsky. Or do I mean 'Robert Pinsky'?

To put it another way, I hope I am still figuring it out, and still working to make a poetry that ambushes, dodges, startles. There's no method for that. And habit is not necessarily one's ally.

On the other hand, I hope that I have become a better reader of myself, a more usefully inventive critic and cheerleader and skeptic toward myself.

Philip Pullman

I have a sense of where the story wants to go, and I help it to get there by, as it were, buying tickets, booking hotel reservations, making appointments. You could call it research if you liked, but that seems a bit too dignified or high-flown for the sort of menial administration that I perform on the story's behalf. The story is the boss. I'm just the servant, the PA, the secretary, the valet, the gentleman's gentleman, the dragoman, the fixer, the pimp.

Tom Shapcott

Each piece of writing is in some way a step into the dark; you have to be prepared for surprises; you have to let the computer of your sub-conscious sometimes lead the way. In order to do that, and to trust that, well you have to have learned the basic elements of your craft. I had published 8 or 9 books of poems before I really tackled prose, and it took quite a number of efforts before I felt I had achieved a sort of prose style that fitted. My second novel was over-planned. It took

6 drafts before I felt I was there (and the published version had several 'characters' who were not in the first – a good example of following, not my plan, but what my subconscious bade me do).

William Tremblay

How much pre-planning goes into your writing process?

Depends on what I'm writing. If it's individual poems in the guilty pleasure of a stolen moment, not much. A person place thing or idea is there on my inner screen begging/demanding attention. A few snapshots. And when that moment opens up no matter where I can fetch my pen and pad and sketch or even catch the wave of a voice that needs to talk about said persons places things or ideas and what I do and don't love about them.

If it's a larger, longer sequence then the whole project is extended and requires longer periods. One could go to Cape Cod and finish a novel, which takes persistence and days, weeks, months. That's where somehow by simply paying attention to the words on this page what comes before shapes what comes next. Or you live at home as you work on a screenplay.

You need a very strong voice of uncertainty if you want to leave things unresolved but that tends to flatten tone out so that many books seem alike. It's as if workshop techniques derive from art studios where students are doing imitations of past art movement styles – Cubism, fauvism, Renaissance Italian, e.g. – where the thinking is all aesthetic. 'I will work in the colour red twice and contradict myself once and use a sequence of numbers and concern myself with adverbs, i.e. with the qualities of action, and I will write to the dying elm in my back yard' could be an example of procedures. You get to think about the items in a procedural list and it frees up the rest of the words to be completely unplanned. Poe said the same thing about rhythm.

Anyway, why be 'ready for things that might occur along the way'? It is good to be blind-sided. It shows you what you didn't know you knew.

Sometimes you need to sleep on it several nights before the next image that will drive the process further as it gets unpacked on the page or screen. I dream holographs, I assume most people do. The greatest inference is depth of field, three dimensionality, given a two dimensional image. And language is way more abstract than even iconic images. 'Mountain shadows make the desert a jagged sundial.'

That sentence just 'came to me' without planning out of the five preceding sentences. This is the way it is for me. For others it is different. *Vive la difference.*

Xu Xi

Well a few things although I always reserve the right to edit my proclamations about anything later! Here's what I know about how I write novels – I generally can't end one until I can clearly see the next one and feel that certainty about its need to be written. I don't quite know why. I know other writers who say, after the last book is out and done, that they now will consider what they might write next and try a few different things. I do that trial while I'm trying to finish a given novel. I am also finding now that each novel takes longer to write than it used to (the average length was four years), probably because I'm less in a hurry to publish than I used to be, which is one of the luxuries of having published several books which are still in print and have gone into new editions, etc. I consider myself lucky on that score. The new novel that's coming out this fall took about 6 years in total (excluding the time when it was a manuscript being shopped around). And the one I'm trying to finish now (that I keep promising my agent I will finish) has taken 8 years so far. I actually think I can finish it now because the new book that's next is very clear to me – I've even been so rash as to talk about it which puts pressure on myself to finish the current one so that I can get to the next.

Other things I know about novels – I will at some point revisit the chronology. I run giant spreadsheets of my novels (have done so for the last three) as I work on them and structure is one of my dreadful obsessions. So dreadful in fact that for my last novel, I deliberately avoided all problems of structure by simply writing a chronological narrative which alternated the storyline of the four main characters. But then by the next book I was juggling structure all over again (the one that's coming out this fall) and the one I'm working on now is a mass of structural contradictions (hence I am now on version 7 of the manuscript).

The other thing is date of birth of my characters. For whatever reason to do with my particular method of working, I simply have to know the year (and sometimes day) everyone was born (even the minor characters – I draw the line at the walk on ones). In some cases, I don't even use a minor character enough so that it should matter, but for me to keep the main characters straight, I need to know their ages relative to the cast of others around them. So my spreadsheet calculates every character's relative position to the others down a y axis based on age. And then I begin to plug in all the potential conflicts, etc. that colour their relationships.

There's always more research, often unexpected. The unpredictability of what will spark forays into obscure or not so obscure knowledge is something I really love about writing novels.

I am far less certain about stories and essays, both of which I also write. They seem to take a different path each time, especially the stories. Essays seem a little more predictable in that I don't tend to sit down to write them until they have taken quite a clear shape in my mind. Stories however I start and abandon constantly – I have a hard drive (and from the past file drawers of paper version) full of partially completed or even completed stories that will probably never see the light of anything.

* * *

Clear, occasionally less clear. Sometimes the task at hand – the *work-in-progress*, that is – plainly defines the direction of things that need doing. Other times, the writer's interviewed in this book return to general ways of working that have evolved over time. That return has implications. For example, Jack Epps Jr. mentions that he has 'an approach that I have used successfully for years'. On the other hand, Kate Grenville suggests that 'the best thing I've learned from having been writing for so long is that it always feels like a failure'. Seemingly time is no guarantee of feeling sure you have successful drafting method. Ruth Padel notes doing 'everything instinctively', while Tom Shapcott feels that 'you have to be prepared for surprises'. For Andy Brown there is not one answer to this question but two: 'I either write poems longhand in notebooks that come all in one go, as an expression of need, or experience, or as an immediate response to something I'm fascinated by and want to explore; or I work on longer-term pieces on the computer.' And William Tremblay comments that it 'depends on what I'm writing'.

If anything is central here it is that drafting links clearly to processes of individual learning. This learning might have occurred to the point where a creative writer feels they have a good general sense of how a project can be approached, even if each project does largely occur anew. This general learning does not always provide specific instruction – there are always questions and there are elements of unknowing that form part of the live-action of us doing our drafting. This *unknowing* might indeed not be a negative element at all.

Because drafting involves learning, and because there is a sense in which previous knowledge is challenged by new writing tasks, it could easily be suggested that what creative writing drafting entails is the meeting of theory and practice.

Theories are principles or explanatory tools. What you know about your ways of drafting can be considered part of your personal theory of creative writing. Simply, this knowledge of your drafting is one of your principles of working, one of your explanatory tools. Understanding of this kind refers back to the combination of thinking and acting that underpins your arts practice. Each individual project, then, brings practice into the realm of theory and, in doing so, raises questions about the theories we have in our minds.

If we step into the dark, if we use others as sounding boards for whether a piece is working or not, if we adopt a structured set of pre-writing activities in order to inform our acts of creative writing, we do so because these particular things form the basis of our personal theory of creative writing. To discover that sometimes we are wrong about how best to proceed might well be one of the primary attractions associated with creative writing. Being wrong suggests there is more to learn and this potentially engages us anew with the formation of ideas about drafting, about creating and about creative writing itself. However, to discover that we are right, or that as creative writers we do have a strong enough combination of understanding and ability to proceed with some confidence, confirms that our abstract reasoning and our experiences have a productive relationship. We discover in this way that our comprehension of how creative writing works remains viable; and, again, this encourages us to continue writing. That fact that *drafting involves both knowing and unknowing* is undoubtedly significant.

Reflection

What do you know about the ways in which you draft your work? Can you list things that, with relative certainty, you *know* will happen? For example, will you plan, will you use a computer in a particular way, will you begin with a sense of the ways in which the story or poem or script will proceed?

Exercise

When drafting, do you have a general sense of the things that you do not know before you begin? This might seem a contradictory question! However, to use an example: if you're currently working on a creative writing project do you sense there are things that are going to come up that you don't currently know? Can you list them now? (suggested word length for this exercise: 300–500 words) Are these issues of subject or theme or form that can be researched, or are they personal ways of working that might come, more so, from your actions (that is, from the act of drafting itself, things connected with the formation of a work but not necessarily with information about a subject or theme or established form)?

Reflection

If in many ways drafting *is* learning then what kind of learner are *you*? Do you prefer to learn via mentoring, one-to-one, or are you more inclined towards that kind of learning that comes from group comparative work, or are you happier with the delivery of information and then some reflective time beyond this to consider that information and its application? These are just a few examples. Perhaps all these, and more, are relevant. Essentially, how we each learn and draft a piece of creative writing could be related closely enough to suggest how we can develop our individual knowledge in, and of, creative writing. That being the case, whether writing on our own or choosing to undertake a creative writing class in a college, university or community setting, we can potentially make better choices about our creative writing if we know how best we learn.

6
Other Creative Writers

Do you ever wonder what other creative writers do as they draft their works? Not in a voyeuristic way, necessarily! I'm thinking more about whether you think 'I wonder if X finds this hard?' Or 'I wonder if Y has a method for dealing with this kind of thing?'

Given the title of his book, *The Place of Writing*,[1] Seamus Heaney appears to be about to deliver a discussion about the environment or, perhaps, about the position creative writing holds in the world, its 'place'. In part he does this. However, what is more fascinating about *The Place of Writing* is that the book concerns itself a great deal with other creative writers.

The Place of Writing 'inaugurated the Richard Ellmann Lectures in Modern literature at Emory University'[2] in 1988 and, indeed, much of what is said by Heaney relates to the circumstances of inauguration and of the connection between Heaney and Ellmann. There is a distinctive history to this book, therefore, and perhaps it is to be expected that what emerges is decidedly personal. And yet, what strikes the reader when encountering the examination of the writing of W.B. Yeats or of Thomas Kinsella, of Louis MacNeice or Michael Longley or of Paul Muldoon, is Heaney's critical interest in the individual.

The Nobel Prize-winning poet grounds his discussion in cultural awareness, his awareness most certainly of Ireland, Irish history and Irish literature, but it would take an enormous amount of will on our behalf not to hear his infinite fascination with other creative writers. He displays that fascination in lines such as this,, concerned with a work by Michael Longley:

> then the poem swerves once more, to hit a panicky note of zany Daliesque hallucination. What are Longley's father's dentures doing here? For here they indisputably are, articulated, effervescent, brilliantly done and grinning.[3]

Heaney goes on to discuss Longley's discovery of some facts and the impact of those facts on the way a poem, entitled 'The Linen Workers', emerged for Longley, but it is the closeness of that action of swerving and the curiosity Heaney has with the choices Longley has made that is most obvious. We can see this in the presence of assessments such as 'panicky' and 'zany' and his conclusion that this has been 'brilliantly done'. This returns us, again and again, to the writer's interest not just in the poem he is discussing but in the making of poetry.

In some other iteration, *The Place of Writing* could have carried the title *The Creating of Writing* because it is in the *creating* that Heaney's personal disposition is located as well as in the creations he mentions. If it is the relationship between history and the imagination, or politics and place, or literature and society that informs some of the discussion in his book, it is his interest in other creative writers that underpins almost all of it. The comments on Longley's 'The Linen Workers' are doubly intriguing because they seem to have Heaney crying out 'Wow, that's an amazing act of poetry writing!' and not a little too: 'How did you manage to accomplish it?'

That is what this question to the creative writers here in *Inside Creative Writing* was about as well. Because creative writing is a human activity and because we cannot help but wonder, every now and then, what it is to be human, it certainly seems possible that we creative writers wonder what it is to be a human who is a creative writer. The question evolves into whether we ever wonder how other creative writers actually *do* their creative writing? If we do wonder, then what is the purpose of our wondering? Is it simple human curiosity or is it a more complex and necessary part of being a creative writer to wonder how other writers do it?

Such wondering could be part of a natural 'group bonding' – the kind of thing that any species does to determine what constitutes the species in the first place. Seamus Heaney's *The Place of Writing* seems to suggest the relationship between the 'doing' in creative writing and a work that is 'done' relates as much to the purpose of establishing that relationship between 'done' and 'doing' as it does to the finished work's existence.

Similarly, identifying with a particular place or group or society might be reason enough to spend time contemplating the actions of those who also occupy the same arena. This would explain why writers' groups, salons, informal creative writing workshops emerge – not just because of a desire to learn skills or create opportunities for distributing works of creative writing but also because creative writers identify with their group, their species (to carry that analogy a little further).

Alternatively, as with anything that involves our physical and mental energy, we might wonder how others best use their personal resources, because this is one way of bolstering our own, and because we know our individual resources are never inexhaustible. Knowing how others allocate their time and effort in the practice of creative writing could be useful to us. If humankind is highly competitive we might wonder if others who undertake creative writing possess some important knowledge that we could use to increase our own level of success at creative writing.

So it might go – if indeed we *do* wonder about other creative writers at all (and that was my query). It could be that we don't. Instead, we write creatively with a personalised sense of the undertaking so that while we might be fascinated by completed works of creative writing (and celebrate the most impressive of these completed works), we pay most attention to how we personally undertake it not to how others undertake it.

* * *

Iain Banks

I suppose I wonder about that kind of thing occasionally, but frankly it's a rather casual pondering. Like most readers I'm just glad that whatever processes went on in the author's head have led to the book that I'm enjoying (and, as I say, I feel I already know the answer to where they get their ideas from).

Charles Baxter

I no longer wonder about other creative writers and their processes, because I know that writing is hard for everybody. Writers are people for whom writing is harder than it is for everyone else.

Andy Brown

I don't think I've ever thought 'I wonder if X finds this hard'; I'm rather more concerned to solve the problems of why *I* might be finding a poem hard myself – that's one of the exciting challenges of every new poem: 'How do I make this work?'; 'How can I do this differently from ways in which I've done it before?'

One does, of course, learn a huge amount from other writers. I'm fascinated by what other writers do, and I try to talk with them about it as much as I can – my professional life has been very kind to me on that score. One poet friend of mine composes entirely 'on the lips', speaking the whole thing through before he writes a single word down. One poet does it all whilst walking, just as the Romantics used to. Another poet I know sounds the whole poem out in terms of musical structures and knows exactly when the *largo* section is coming; when the *prestissimo*. These little gems of others' practice are remarkably durable and valuable.

Isn't it intriguing when a poet tells you *how* they do what they do? I think you can learn from them in three main ways. Firstly, you can read their poems and work out how the poem works; what the poet is doing with the language. This is learning-to-read-like-a-writer (and to write-like-a-reader) and once you've crossed this conceptual bridge there's no going back. Whilst it's absolutely vital to do this, it can be a bit like a magician telling you how the illusion is performed, so the trick is to be able to recognise technique and craft without that knowledge crushing the sensory and emotional pleasure of the poem. Secondly, I think, you can talk with the writer him or herself, which is why it's important to be involved with writers and readers and events and the wider worlds of writing. And thirdly, you can read interviews like this. The most important way in which you'll learn, however, is by doing the writing yourself; by immersing yourself in the processes of writing and working these things through for yourself. It doesn't matter if it doesn't lead to a published poem each time: it's the process that matters. Beckett sums it up succinctly of course: 'Fail. Fail again. Fail better.'

Maggie Butt

Not really. When I am writing, I'm lost in it, wholly concentrated on it. But I do feel envy of other writers for the work they produce, and a desire to try harder, to get better.

Jack Epps Jr.

Not really. I have my methods and what someone else does is more of a curiosity. I do believe that everyone needs to find their own approach. What works for me, might not work for you. Richard Shepherd, THE MATADOR, likes to start on page one and start typing and see what happens. He does that for several drafts. John August, BIG FISH, likes to write scenes out of order. He writes the scene he feels like writing. I could never do that since each scene depends on the previous scene for emotional continuity.

But it doesn't matter. It's what gets you into the heart of your material the quickest and the deepest.

As a novice, I did spend a great deal of time studying the approaches of other writers and experimented until I found my own method. Rob Thompson, HEARTS OF THE WEST, first told me about the index card method which I quickly adapted. William Goldman said in an interview that he goes to his office every day whether he is writing or not. He approaches it as a professional – it's a job and you go ready to work. I adopted that approach to writing. It's not about inspiration – it's about perspiration. John Milias said, 'I write the movies I like to see on the screen.' That sort of liberated me to trust my instincts and write my movies instead of chasing someone else's movie that I admired.

But once a writer approaches their work enough, and has a degree of success, they stay with what works, and that's where I am. I know how to break a story – it's still not easy – and then once I know it, I know how to get it down. That's not going to change.

Nadine Gordimer

There's no methodology for fiction.

Kate Grenville

It was very helpful to work on a book with Sue Woolfe called *Making Stories* – we found early drafts and compared them with the published version, then interviewed the writers about what happened in between. I learned a lot – about taking notes, about using index cards, about listening to the voice that says, chuck this out, it's boring.

Nessa O'Mahony

I always assume that nobody else has problems at all, and that I'm the only one who does!

Ruth Padel

Sometimes I'm interested to hear how my friends do things – but more interested in the final products.

Robert Pinsky

I have been blessed with very good friends in writing. So I have some idea how Bob Hass or Louise Glück or Charlie Williams might deal with something. As creative writing students perhaps do with one another.

Having never taken a proper creative writing course (though I now teach them), I feel I have had the equivalent, thanks to so many excellent and generous friends in the art. Working with Bob and Czeslaw Milosz on English versions of Czeslaw's poems was a creative writing course for me.

Philip Pullman

No. I know how I do it, and I don't care how X does it.

Tom Shapcott

In teaching I have come across many false starts, and have, I think, assisted in redirecting the author to more fertile lines of inquiry or process. I have been much influenced in the achievements of other writers, but not necessarily in their various drafting processes, though it is always interesting to see these (Eliot's 'The Waste Land' is the great example, though in Australia I happened to be at the National Library in Canberra when the Kenneth Slessor archive arrived, and I could see in his great bound drafting books the various permutations 'Five Bells', his famous long poem, went through. That was less a learning experience than idle curiosity.

William Tremblay

I wonder if X has a method for dealing with this kind of thing?

Of course. You wake up to a day with no energy and you face the page and you have fantasies about pumping out someone else's brains for what you don't have enough hunger for to invent yourself.

It is tempting to think that if only you had an inexhaustible method you would never fall by the wayside panting. It is also tempting to think that just as professional athletes have personal trainers there would be a person in your life who would drive you to produce or give you the keys to producing production.

Again, here, if you're writing in the long form you have time to see the jewel of your story: *A man's father teaches him how to go safely invisible but he risks being visible for the woman he loves.* That is the logline of the adaptation of my novel I'm working on. It's brief; I don't know yet if it conveys foreboding or invitation or both.

Xu Xi

I almost hate to admit this but I have NEVER thought about how other writers solve their writing problems. I have always operated on the principle that my writing process is something I need to figure out and what anyone else does is not necessarily what will best inform my learning. I am fundamentally a trial and error person, which is probably why it took me so long to figure out what kind of writer I was really trying to be. But you can't change character, not really; at most

I have become more efficient. And as a teacher of creative writing, I do suggest that students look for efficient models and approaches in their own creative process (I might not feel that way if I taught mostly undergrad age students, but mine are often older adult learners, and I do feel they don't have all the time in the world so I try my best to veer them away from what might be less productive approaches, e.g.: taking three years to research some tiny detail because that suggests the work probably is more about the tiny detail than the writer is willing to acknowledge, etc.

*   *   *

If completed works of creative writing – the books, the poems, the television shows, the plays, the digital works and so on – do reveal something of the creative writing undertaken as well as something of the creative writer's actions along the way, then just as certainly a great deal about creative writing practice remains hidden in these completed works. Nevertheless, it is far from suggested by the evidence in the answers here that starting with a consideration of how other creative writers do their creative writing, solve their writing problems, complete the tasks they set themselves, is the solution.

Nessa O'Mahony assumes 'that nobody else has problems at all, and that I'm the only one who does', and that comment might well be reflective of how each of us come to terms with our own creative writing. It's not unlike Andy Brown's quoting of Samuel Beckett: 'Fail. Fail again. Fail better.' While we can all recognise that completing a piece of work involves solving problems, these problems seem too personalised to be subject to general, transferable solutions. Not that a creative writer will never think about the possibility of transferable solutions, of course; but that thinking can often be more like Iain Banks' 'rather casual pondering', or like the sort of thing that Robert Pinsky and Ruth Padel talk about when they talk about sharing thoughts with friends. In some cases, though, there are specific bridges between what we are encountering individually as creative writers and what other creative writers are encountering. For example, Tom Shapcott mentions that in teaching he has 'come across many false starts' and Xu Xi suggests to students that they 'look for efficient models and approaches in their own creative process'. But equally, as Nadine Gordimer notes in relation to fiction writing, there may be 'no methodology' or, as Charles Baxter puts it, 'writing is hard for everybody'.

It's tempting to speculate on whether, if were we talking about a different field of endeavour, these answers to the question of wondering about how others do it would be the same? There's probably not a right or wrong to that question, but what comes to mind is how we generally locate creative writing as something that others do, as well as something that we do.

Our societal interest in the hidden actions of creative writing composition is revealed in our preservation of writers' manuscripts and diaries and notebooks and drafts – a whole gamut of literary archiving that has gone on for centuries and that declares the value we place on this evidence of writerly practice. And yet, of course, it is not *every* writer's work that we preserve, not every manuscript or diary that finds its way into a library or a museum.

The value of this material, in this sense, is defined by prevailing cultural conditions as well as by prevailing critical opinion and, perhaps less obviously, by the fortuitous circumstances of a creative writer's life that raises the profile of one creative writer but not another, that brings attention to one completed work but not another. In this way, notions of value underlie how we are offered evidence of the practice of creative writing, how that evidence is preserved and presented, and how we are given access to it.

But what was asked of the creative writers here was located in the intuitive, more related to their problem-solving. On reading the responses it feels as though an attached question about particular creative writing practices might be asked. So, for example, if we struggle creating a character in a novel we could ask ourselves if another writer, whose work with character is strong, ever felt the same way. We could institute a 'strengths' and 'weaknesses' approach, and ask ourselves if there are things that we feel are difficult and those that we feel are easier. Additionally, we could ask if a reader or audience notices the things with which we had difficulty or if these are no more visible (or invisible) than any other creative writing practice.

What comes to mind finally is the voice of Seamus Heaney in *The Place of Writing* when he says, in a lecture on W.B. Yeats:

> One of the first functions of a poem, after all, is to satisfy a need in the poet. The achievement of sufficient form and release of a self-given music have a justifying effect within his life. And if the horizons inside which that life is being lived are menacing, the need for the steadying gift of finished art becomes all the more urgent.[4]

As we locate our undertaking of creative writing in our needs as well as our desires we come back to questions about the pragmatics of doing creative writing. Ultimately, in times of difficulty, we rightly draw on methods of working that best seem to support us. If we can correctly identify these, that will always be to our advantage.

Reflection

Why not seek out the manuscripts of another creative writer, the diaries, the letters, the evidence in any form? Make this perhaps a casual, personal seeking, in a library or archive. No definite research methodology, no specific inference to the seeking – other than to informally ask if there is anything that is revealed to you that might be of general or specific use?

Exercise

Do you find some things hard about creative writing and other things not so hard? Do you have expectations about this, and find they are always met – for example, knowing that creating your desired structure in a poem will be more difficult than actually finding the subject or theme to write about? Have you a 'Top 3' of your common writing difficulties? Set these out and explain why you think these are your common difficulties (suggested word length for this exercise: 750–1000 words). If you could list all the things that are likely to slow you up, concern you, or even prevent you finishing a piece of creative writing, is it possible to suggest solutions for any of the major impediments? (add another 500–750 words on this).

Reflection

Finally, if have you a creative writer or creative writers you most admire, and you could ask them anything at all about how they undertake their creative writing, what would it be?

7
Creative Work-in-Progress

Apart from when someone interrupts you with questions such as these (with apologies!), do you talk much about your work? Do you talk to other creative writers regularly? I guess there's also the question about impacting on works that are not yet complete. More particularly, then, do you ever talk about 'work-in-progress' – with anyone?

There's an educational turn to this chapter and to this question, and it bears some initial examining because it will help us to focus on issues that arise around what is commonly called 'work-in-progress'. Before even reading the creative writers' responses, we should recall this: almost all the work undertaken in universities and colleges in the field of creative writing relies on someone, some time, showing a creative writing work-in-progress to someone else. The same could be said, in fact, about creative writing undertaken in schools or community education settings. As soon as we concentrate on the teaching and learning of creative writing the idea of *not* showing someone a work *until* it is completed becomes fraught with issues. This need not entirely be the case.

A creative writing course can involve the introduction to, and exploration of, forms and techniques and ideas and concepts and the work submitted for the course can be submitted at its conclusion. A record of a student having achieved can be located in how this submitted work reveals what has been learnt. There is evidence of a version of this approach, broadly speaking, in other fields of study. That is: you learn the material, apply the techniques to your own project outside of the classroom, and you present that project at the end of the course.

So maybe that kind of approach could occur in creative writing teaching. But largely it doesn't, and for very good reason. After all, one potential problem with such an approach lies in how to advise a creative writing learner on specific issues of composition, general skill or specific technique – that is, if their project is not seen until it is submitted. Some aspects of composition, skill and technique might be shown with reference to pieces of finished creative writing (most obviously the published works of other writers), but a directly relevant example is harder to come by if the student's work-in-progress is being undertaken out of sight.

Because a student writer's own work offers the very best opportunity for a relevant discussion, work-in-progress exchanges are often key moments in university or college creative writing workshops. Both learner and teacher rely upon them. But the query (and the issue indirectly posed to the creative writers in *Inside Creative Writing* also) is how close is that situation to the reality of a creative writer's working life outside a classroom?

Another, more complex consideration in creative writing teaching and learning relates to judging how far a student has progressed from the point of starting a creative writing course to the point of finishing it. Although this issue is not unique to creative writing, the problem is enhanced by the range of potential influences a creative writer can encounter. Even focusing only on creative writing technique this can be the case. For example, being a good creator of narrative does not necessarily mean you will be automatically good at word choice, understanding rhythm does not necessarily mean you will be closely engaged with image, and so on.

Creative writing draws from such a substantial gamut of knowledge – cognitive (that is, mental processing), aesthetic, physical, language-based... knowledge – such a gamut that progress in it is not single-paced. Work-in-progress exchanges therefore offer a conceptual (ways of thinking) and a material (ways of acting) grounding, an avenue along which the learner and teacher can share a sense of how things are developing, and a method for locating any issues across a range of learning.

The role of consciousness, and self-consciousness, in creative writing also emerges. Consciousness involves our awareness and our perception of surroundings and of ourselves, our attentiveness. Self-consciousness, however, involves too great an awareness of our appearance or our actions; in other words, an over-abundance that can thwart a balanced relationship between us and our surroundings, between our actions and how those actions are perceived.

Creative writing work-in-progress can be understood as finely balanced between these two states – our conscious appreciation of creating something, but the potentially self-conscious recognition that this creation hasn't received our final approval. Because work-in-progress involves pieces of creative writing we *might* be willing to release to others in some fashion, but are also considered not universally ready, work-in-progress exists in something of a half-world. This half-world is not unimportant, it is not inconsequential: it contains evidence of our personalities, our histories, our social, cultural and professional contexts. Work-in-progress also contains our judgements.

When we are writing, we are employing several archetypes of judgement simultaneously, and not only as pertains to creative writing itself. For example, there are our judgements about our way of creating. Do we believe we most often write something that is within reach of a final draft, or is it more likely that some major changes will occur towards the end of the making of the work? There are judgements too about how much our internal assessment of what is successful and what is not successful is impacted upon by external opinion. Quite obviously, we could point to aspects of self-awareness, to our periods of confidence, or lack of confidence, or even of over-confidence.

Other judgements can include those concerned with professionalism – so, the creative writer who keeps his or her work-in-progress to a small trusted group in recognition of the fact that, culturally, it is assumed that the difference between the professional artist and the amateur artist is that the professional artist doesn't struggle as much to perfect a work (however true or untrue that might be!). Also, deciding whether to expose work-in-progress to others might involve purely pragmatic aspects, such as showing a work-in-progress to an editor to assure them that, yes indeed, the work is moving along and will be finished by the agreed deadline.

These are just a few scenarios. What constitutes a work-in-progress, who sees it, how it is used, and how any opinions on it are put in context by the writer, involves the disposition (that is, temperament) of the writer as well as the compositional context that the creative writer encounters. If discussion of works-in-progress did not turn out to be present for *any* of the writers here in *Inside Creative Writing*, it would not necessarily reflect negatively on the fact that for some time teaching and learning in creative writing has involved work-in-progress exchanges and many creative writing programmes (including the ubiquitous creative writing workshop) rely on work-in-progress discussions.

Had that been the case, it could well have been a matter of who was interviewed here rather than a general consensus. Fourteen writers is a good cross-section, but still relatively small as a 'survey group'. Fortunately, the creative writers in *Inside Creative Writing* do offer a range of opinions on work-in-progress discussions and, though not all of the writers undertake these discussions, the question of what takes place draws out some useful thoughts about our own actions, and about our responses to our progress.

* * *

Iain Banks

I used to talk more about my books when I was in the middle of them, but I don't usually bother much these days; I'm more confident that I know how it's going without getting an outside opinion and most people don't want to have any surprises spoiled for them. Well, that's what they tell me, anyway. Generally, though, I'm quite relaxed about talking about a work in progress. I talk to other writers occasionally, though we usually touch on writing only briefly.

Charles Baxter

Self-consciousness is the enemy of creativity, and I try to keep such conversations to a minimum. Most of the time, the only conversations I have about works-in-progress are those I have with myself.

Andy Brown

Yes, I get to talk about my own work a good deal, as a teacher and, more often than not, after I've given a poetry reading. It's a very good thing to be asked to talk through your ideas about what it is *you think you are doing* when you write. I ask students to do it all the time, so why shouldn't I be forced to do it as well? Talking with, and listening to others, in any walk of life, is always good advice I would say: it stops you falling in love with the sound of your own voice, and may even persuade you that there are other valid opinions about poetry (including your own poetry). Poets are notoriously poor critics of their own poems.

Talking about work-in-progress is slightly different and some writers are superstitious about it. I have the unpleasant feeling that I've jinxed a couple of my previous projects by talking about them (in print) before they were completed and accepted for publication. When they subsequently remained unpublished, it was a salutary lesson in keeping my mouth shut.

Maggie Butt

I have a couple of trusted poet friends whose feedback on draft poems is always useful, even if I disagree with it and thereby discover my own direction. I also belong to a Poetry Society Stanza group, which meets monthly, in which we share our poems-in-progress and get a good range of responses and suggestions. It's a very supportive and egalitarian group, with no massive egos and lots of good ideas.

When I wrote two novels as part of a PhD I greatly enjoyed talking to my supervisors about the process and direction of the work. It was hugely helpful to me. They were well informed, well read, and actually paid to have the time to be interested!

Jack Epps Jr.

I was in a partnership for a very long time and we talked about every aspect of our work daily. It was really helpful to get to the work quickly. But we never talked to anyone else about story development unless we were forced to by contract.

Now I write alone – harder and not as much fun – other than to pitch the idea, I don't like to talk it out before I write it. I think creative ideas are very fragile and there is a danger that someone won't get it. They will say something that crushes the butterfly. So, I like to talk to the page. Work out my questions by writing it out. Then, once I have a draft I give it only to people I trust, who I know will give me constructive feedback. It's important not to give your work to just anyone, because you might get just any crazy note that can throw you off for a very long time. But it is important to give your work to several people. If they are all saying the same thing, then you need to try and find a way to solve that problem.

Mario Puzo, *The Godfather*, had a rule that I adopted. Don't talk your story out – don't tell it to anyone. Write it out on the page. Save the story telling for the page. If you talk it out too much, you'll lose the energy. I want to hit the page excited and curious to find out how it's going to write.

Nadine Gordimer

I never talk about work in progress or read parts to anyone. Of course I talk to comrade writers who also are my friends. Apart from our shared interests in other manifestations of being alive, I have special joy in explaining what their works mean to me, when I respond to them. My enthusiasm for achievement and any criticisms, if I have any. I celebrate their books, part of the endless single volume we are trying to find and of the mystery of life.

Kate Grenville

As I said earlier, there's a long time with a book where no-one can help you with it. Many of my friends are writers, but we don't talk much about what we're working on – just rarely, when there might be a particular specific problem. In my experience writers together tend to whinge about their publishers and compare notes on their agents.

Being alone with the problem for me is the best as well as the worst thing about writing. It's remarkable, though, how unrelated conversations have a way of feeding into the writing in an oblique way.

Nessa O'Mahony

I find myself in the workshop scenario quite often. It's mostly as a facilitator, these days, although I thoroughly enjoy the process of being a participant as well. So there's lots of discussion about ways of doing things, which I find quite natural and normal. I was also a member of an online community for a while, which involved posting work in progress online for commentary. I found that quite a useful sounding-board. I'm also a member of a monthly workshop where very experienced women writers come together to read and critique; that's been an enormously helpful experience as I'm always aiming to produce a draft that nobody has anything to criticise about. It hasn't happened yet.

Ruth Padel

Yes – other writers. Most poets have people they might show problems poems to – other poets whose work they admire and judgement they trust.

Robert Pinsky

Poets – American poets, anyway – seem to do this quite a lot. Fiction writers, climbing while carrying their complicated object up so many inclines, seem more likely to prefer no company until they've reached the summit. I share drafts with the poets I mentioned above, and many more. With the early drafts of my Inferno, Seamus Heaney, who was living here at the time, helped quite a lot. Today, David Ferry showed me some striking new poems he is working on, and we worried at relative pronouns and such in one of them.

Philip Pullman

Only very occasionally, with David Fickling, my editor of over twenty years' standing; but I don't always tell him the truth. Otherwise never. A good servant (see no. 5 [Question 5]) should not betray his master's secrets. But, you know, I don't think writers talk to each other much about what they're writing. Film people talk about it all the time. Conversations and discussions are endless, because everybody has a stake in how the story will develop; and a whole language has grown up about arcs and back-stories and second-act climaxes and so on, to make the conversation easier; but the end result is usually no good, despite all of that. Film is a collaborative process anyway by its nature – you have to talk about what you're doing. But writing a novel isn't. It *should* be private, is my view. It is almost inexpressible. To talk about it spoils more than it helps.

Tom Shapcott

Rodney Hall and I used regularly, as beginner writers, to show each other work-in-progress. And other personal writer friends, have given feedback, though usually at a much later stage (David Malouf, though, saw much of my early prose). It is very helpful for a beginning writer. The older you get, though, perhaps you are more set in your ways. You might claim you know what you are after, but there is always the danger of ossification. I have always experimented with the wide range of forms, but I do have less sympathy these days with experimentation for its own sake. Perhaps that is another way of saying I am now more interested in what is being said than how it is said.

William Tremblay

Do you talk about works-in-progress with anyone?

Yes, happily. I have several friends with whom I have shared a lot of phone time talking about writing projects. They don't offer concrete solutions to my writing fears, roadblocks, boundaries or wounds but make sympathetic sounds over the wire, enough for me to realize how much of a burden of ineffability I'm putting them under. We are a community by virtue of what we give each other.

Xu Xi

I only talk about works in progress with non writers. Because I have been teaching creative writing in recent years, I do talk about process and works in progress a whole lot more with writers than I ever used to. But here's an interesting distinction – I will reveal to non-writer acquaintances details of what I'm working on that I would never tell students or another writer, even those who are pretty good friends with whom I regularly have literary exchanges about a whole host of things. Don't quite know why.

* * *

Context is a difficult bedfellow! Take these two points of view: firstly, that a creative writer's work-in-progress is more likely to be shown to others early in their careers, when they are exploring the level of their skill; secondly, that a creative writer's work-in-progress is more likely to be shown to others later in their careers, when they are more confident in their judgements.

One, or neither, of these points of view might be true! Similarly, if we show work to others only sometimes, or only to non-writers, or in no particular pattern at all of 'creating-receiving responses-creating', does this mean that work-in-progress has an indeterminate place in the actions of creative writing? Considering the views of the writers here, the general answer would seem to be that work-in-progress can work for us as a private conversation with others. Consensus seems to suggest that while a continual, never-ending conversation would be merely noise a pertinent, private conversation is relatively common.

For Philip Pullman work-in-progress discussions occur 'only very occasionally' and Nadine Gordimer never talks 'about work in progress or read parts to anyone'. Iain Banks says he's changed his approach over time and is now 'more confident that I know how it's going without getting an outside opinion'. Maggie Butt has 'a couple of trusted poet friends whose feedback on draft poems is always useful'. Robert Pinsky makes the more general point that in terms of discussing work-in progress 'poets – American poets, anyway – seem to do this quite a lot. Fiction writers, climbing while carrying their complicated object up so many inclines, seem more likely to prefer no company until they've reached the summit'.

These answers do not necessarily send the message: 'whatever works for you, do that!' Rather, what decisions about revealing work-in-progress attach themselves to is what we can call *convergence*. The sharing of work-in-progress can be part of a convergence of ideals and attitudes – such as in the case of showing work to friends or close colleagues. It can be part of convergence in the sense of teaching and learning, so that something is shared across what is known and what is not yet known, between people participating in an educational endeavour. And sharing work-in-progress can constitute convergence in the sense of the event of writing and the writer's life, so that some particular emotional or professional situation initiates a desire to share and discuss unfinished work.

Reflection

Do you have a work-in-progress that you are willing, or even keen, to show to others? Assuming you do have a work-in-progress why, or why not, would you show it to others? To whom would you show it?

Exercise

Have you ever shown an unfinished work to someone and found their response helpful or unhelpful? Briefly (suggested word length for this exercise: no more than 200 words) what was good, or bad, about their response? Was this in a formal creative writing class or in some other informal circumstance? How much did the situation or environment impact their responses? Did you go on to finish the work?

Reflection

What would be your ideal situation if you were to show someone a work-in-progress? Why would this be ideal?

8
Creative Writing Habitats

Quite a few creative writers mention places, and circum-
stances, where they write best. Is that the case for you, or
could you write almost anywhere, almost any time? Possibly
if you answer positively to the second part of this question,
you'll hear some deafening groans/sighs of envy!

To ask where we work best is both a philosophic and a pragmatic
question. On the one hand, where we work reveals something
of how we each situate ourselves in the world, our perceived
relations with our surroundings, and with other people, even
the relationship we envisage between our private thoughts
and our public actions of writing. On the other hand, asking
where we work best can be explored by talking about places
that aid our concentration, or the type of instrument we use to
write also reflects the wider methods by which we compose our
works, and that too is *both* a pragmatic and a philosophic consideration. Considering space and place is therefore of interest
in understanding what stimulates and supports us when we're
undertaking creative writing. But, of course, this stimulation
and support is not only about place: creative writing also occurs
within time.

As a physical act creative writing has duration. That is, the
physical act of writing takes place over a certain length of
time. Interestingly, throughout history this has been one of
the most common ways individual creative writers have moni-
tored their writing, mapping how much they have written onto

how long it has taken them to write it. This kind of equation is associated with a writer's personal work ethic, and this work ethic may not necessarily be specific to creative writing. Likewise, this situation with creative writing is not dissimilar to other instances where someone is working in any field independent of a formal, contractual working day; where they are self-employed, dependent on their own assessment of what is a reasonable amount of working effort. We could explore this further, but it would take us a little far from the question posed here in this chapter.

Culturally, certain writing forms have historically established what we can call 'durational recognition'. That is, we've come to associate them, and recognise them, according to certain durations of writerly effort. A good example: the novel form has often been associated with a long effort, even if some novels have not actually taken their writers more time to compose than a short story or a poem. The novel form's 'durational recognition' might thus sometimes be inaccurate – for one creative writer or another. But the notion that the writing a novel involves a long effort is widely shared and culturally touted, regardless.

As with much art making, time taken and results observed have a fairly indirect association. Simply put, no one can ever expect that because they have put in the hours they will naturally produce the best results. Even if that were the case in all other fields of human endeavour – which it is not – it certainly is not the case in creative writing. Broadly speaking, though, the communal sense of what it means to be a creative writer has often been portrayed in terms of doing it regularly. Regardless of whether inspiration is a random occurrence or whether our imaginations have any relationship with duration, the modern consensus about 'being a writer' remains fairly well situated in not just writing occasionally, not just doing it when the mood strikes you, but in doing it at least regularly enough to fill a good portion of your time.

One of the mainstays of books on creative writing, books providing advice to budding creative writers, has indeed been the recommendation that a creative writer needs to write regularly. A great number of these books even suggest that a person wishing to be a creative writer needs to write every day, even if only for a short period. Unquestionably, it would be wrong to say that the amount of effort any of us applies to any endeavour is not a significant factor in our successes – but, the suggestion that time spent relates directly to results achieved is not supported by the evidence.

That said, place and time are practically influential in creative writing. Place and time form part of a creative writer's 'habitat'. Habitats are not merely physical spaces, they also incorporate ways of behaving and ways of responding to that which is around you. Habitats can be largely adopted (that is, we enter somewhere but we don't change it very much) or they can be adapted (that is, we change and develop a habitat to more closely resemble what we require). A habitat is generally defined as a place where someone or something is mostly like to be found.[1]

Specific examples are best left to the comments of the interviewed writers; therefore, at this point, merely some summary, general observations. A creative writer's habitat can be a stable domestic location, and all their work might be undertaken there. Read any of the great number of literary biographies or autobiographies and you'll read of a writer's home, of the room or desk where they write. Alternatively, habitats can be adopted for particular projects at particular times. Writing form and genre contribute something to this; after all, the writing of certain genre actively encourages travel or relocation. Perhaps part of the attraction for some of us creative writers is exactly that kind of habitat change!

Equally, an individual writer's choice of how to explore facts (what methods to use for this), how to engage with a subject or theme, determines how much their habitat might reflect their methods of investigation. Your habitat reflects your actions, and researching is an action. Researching for creative writing is not fixed by any particular paradigm, even though creative writers often draw on many other fields of understanding and their modes of investigation. A creative writer might draw from the field of history or from the field of natural science, from the action research processes seen in many social sciences, or from the textual examinations of many of the humanities – just to name a few possible fields.

In those fields there are shared traditions, if not fixed ideas, about how to undertake investigations. But creative writing is an art – if we deal with facts at all, how we discover them, how we use them and how we convey them, is particularised and variable. Our habitats reflect this. The creative writer who sits at home and explores an imaginary world, appearing to use only the barest of empirical evidence (that is, material gained through observation), is at least as common, if not more common, as the writer who sets off to explore the world through direct and recorded observation. More will be said about this in Chapter 9.

'Where do you write?', 'When do you write?' are in this way references to a particular set of writerly actions and to a particular art form. They are also references to our individual circumstances and to a relationship between pragmatic and philosophic considerations. A wider study of creative writers, involving more writers and a longer period of investigation, might reveal that creative writing most often occurs in certain places and at certain times. Researchers could explore whether there are psychological or physiological reasons why this is the case. Such a study would no doubt point to historical conditions – for example, a change in creative writing habitats brought about by the arrival of the personal computer in the latter half of the twentieth century.

Finally, just as a change of writing tools can impact upon the *where* and *when* of creative writing, so our cultural beliefs have an impact upon the time and space of creative writing in many ways. Investigations of this kind would unearth a great deal about creative writing, but they have not yet been undertaken. However, a good starting point for them would be the comments of individual creative writers, such as those that follow.

*   *   *

Iain Banks

I can write on the hoof but I prefer to write at home in my study. I only write for two or three months of the year and I'm very good at giving myself days off if the weather's nice, so it's not much of a restriction.

Charles Baxter

I need daylight. I tried writing in a room without windows and found that I couldn't do it. Mornings are the best time for me, because that's when I'm alert. These days, I usually write at a desk with a window to my left, and a wall in front of me, on which is pinned a poster of a painting by Paul Klee.

Andy Brown

I have neither a particular time nor a particular place in which I write best. It's always simply been a case of fitting it in around my professional and personal responsibilities. Of course, the making and collating of notes can happen at any time, anywhere (always try and carry a notebook!) and the reading and research that is also a big part of writing is also ongoing all of the time: I tend to do a lot of reading and writing when I'm travelling. But the actual re-drafting, nuts-and-bolts, hard work of sitting down to shape those words on your sheet of A4, that only happens when I can fit it in, sitting down at home (and permitting myself the luxury of ignoring the phone).

When I was Centre Directing for Arvon, I could only write late at night – between 10p.m. and 2a.m. – because of the time constraints of the job, and also at the weekends if I could bear to. When I was a classroom teacher, I used to write manically during the holidays, then write nothing for the next 12 weeks whilst I was teaching in term time, only editing the last batch of material during the subsequent holidays. I more or less have to do that now with my University post: I write avidly (and without any specific purpose other than getting material down) during the Christmas and Easter holidays, and do a good deal of re-drafting, editing and shaping over the summer holidays. The other absolute luxury of the University post is the blessed sabbatical! Every three-and-a-half years I've been granted a semester's Research Leave to develop and finish a new book. These extended periods of time are a godsend: time in which to read, remember who you are, and what is important to you, and to explore that on the page, with purposeful publication in mind. I can't think of a luckier job.

Maggie Butt

I've never understood those people who write in cafes. I'm much too nosey, I'd just be transcribing other people's conversations. And eating too much.

I have to have silence to write. And preferably be alone in the house. That's quite hard to arrange with earning a living and having a family, so I get up when everyone else is still sleeping at the weekend, and write then. Though that's a struggle because I love to sleep too.

Ideas and first phrases happen anywhere, at any time – usually the most inconvenient possible, like driving the car, or in the bath.

Jack Epps Jr.

I have written a ton so I am comfortable writing almost anywhere – but it's more about mental clarity, preparation, and attack, than location. I need to be ready to write – get all the distractions out of the way. I need long blocks of uninterrupted time to get into the zone. I don't want to be interrupted by phone calls or email, or anything that will break the trance.

So, rather than a place, it's more a state of mind. And to have the right state of mind, I need to be ready to write and not be disturbed. I can't write on a plane because there are too many distractions. I write at home in my office because I can shut the door and be left alone for long periods of time. It's getting into the groove that counts. And you can't just write one day, turn it off, then turn it back on. You need to block out large blocks of time where you can finish the work. Even if it's as little as 2 hours a day, you need to own those 2 hours and not let anything disturb you.

John Grisham, *The Firm*, was the kind of writer I always wanted to be. Get up at 4 AM – write before going to work. Very disciplined. I just enjoy my sleep too much. I write in blocks during the day. Take breaks. Let it sort of build up, and then work another block at night. The key is to be undisturbed, turn off the phones, unplug the internet. The internet is the biggest danger to a writer. Every email answered is writing. It drains the good writing. Turn it off.

Nadine Gordimer

No. I can only write – so far in my long life – at home, 'living' wherever it is my characters do, how they do.

Kate Grenville

I've always written around paid work and/or young children, so I do seem to be able to write pretty much under most circumstances. You just can't wait for the time & place to be right, and if you only have 10 minutes you just have to use them.

Once the kids were at school I found the rhythm of the school day, week and year quite a good one for a writer – it was sometimes maddening to have to down pen in time for the school pickup, but much more often the break and engagement with them and their world was hugely rewarding – not just personally but for the work as well. So much of what I've written came out of what you could think of as the 'interruptions' – in fact, the interruptions were the real creative engine.

Taking a quick note on the back on an envelope is something I've always done – in line with my idea that you don't have to get it right first off – you can start with a few words taken on the run and trust that eventually that will be of use.

Nessa O'Mahony

I used to be able to write anywhere, although not now. I think it's a question of head-space, rather than physical environment. I'm a responsive writer so tend to get depressed if I don't have anything to respond to. But one can get too much of a good thing. I once spent a month in a writer's retreat in California and was appalled to discover that I had 24 hours a day available to me to write. I didn't know what to do with myself.

Ruth Padel

Anywhere. Cafes, libraries, aeroplanes.

Robert Pinsky

I like to work whenever it's inconvenient.

(Too much calm, light and lovely ambience can give me stage-fright.)

Philip Pullman

Well, I have written in all sorts of places, and if the need arose I dare say I could do so again; but habit is a great friend. I like going to the same room every day and knowing, without looking, how far I have to stretch my arm to pick up the dictionary; things like that. It saves effort.

Tom Shapcott

When my kids were growing, I think I could write anywhere. Like the kitchen table, where the composer Dvorak, reputedly did his composing. But I often retreated to a favourite chair. On the other hand, in the days when I was a Public Accountant, I frequently had a half-written poem under the Financial Statements I was preparing! I am now retired, so I have all the time in the world. When I was Professor of creative writing, I actually wrote a tremendous amount of my own stuff, but I do not know if I could have kept that up forever. See my comments on 'persistence' however.

William Tremblay

Do you have a best place or can you write anywhere?

I write wherever I am. I have a laptop.

Xu Xi

At a desk, in a quiet place far away from people I know, early in the morning. Which means I would never get anything done if I only wrote in such circumstances. I write in bed on my laptop, in my office space at my various homes (in New York, Hong Kong and New Zealand – now this last is the quiet one but I won't get there for awhile now thanks to my job at City University), have done so at writer's residencies often with great success, onboard planes, in waiting lounges. The one place I try NOT to write in is coffee shops/cafes because there are some clichès I wish to avoid. I will however write in some bars, but not very many. As for time of day, about 15–20 years ago or thereabouts, I *made* myself learn to write at times other than the morning, which has always been my preferred time. Partly this was because my corporate life was pushing me up the ladder (towards that level of eventual incompetence that allowed me to leave that life) and the 40 hour week was ballooning into the 50, then 60, then 70 and even 80 hour week; later a lot of business travel got in (65 to 70% of the time on the road) and so I told myself that if I was going to keep turning out work, I would have to learn to write at whatever time I could snatch out of the day. And so I did and now if I have a choice, I'll write in the mornings, but I can also write at other times of the day much more easily than I used to. Necessity as mother of the inventive life, yes indeed.

* * *

Generally speaking, very few creative writers will have daily lives that mean they only have to write. Most creative writers do other things alongside their writing, by necessity or by choice. There are fewer writers still who don't find something of their general lives intersecting with something of their daily writing plans. That is why those books that say 'a writer must write regularly' are fine in principle but can be a little worrying in practice. What appears to determine our ability to undertake creative writing is mostly a strong enough yearning within us to do it. This goes beyond any specific writerly need we might have, even if the writer has personal preferences for a writing time and a writing place.

So when Ruth Padel says she can write 'anywhere. Cafes, libraries, aeroplanes' this also reflects aspects of her life beyond those place and time choices for writing. And these are quite different, as we see, to those of Nadine Gordimer who says she can 'only write – so far in my long life – at home' and different again from Xu Xi who says she prefers to write 'at a desk, in a quiet place far away from people I know, early in the morning. In addition, we might not write in the same place, and for the same periods, throughout our writing lives. Tom Shapcott notes that 'when my kids were growing' he 'could write anywhere. Like the kitchen table, where the composer Dvorak, reputedly did his composing. Though he also notes that he 'often retreated to a favourite chair'. That aspects of habitat – the smaller spaces, the specific locations within a room – frequently determines how we situate ourselves as writers. And in quite personal ways, as we see in Robert Pinsky's comment that 'too much calm, light and lovely ambience can give me stage-fright.'

One intriguing thought is to wonder when in life we best learn and develop our creative writing – if, indeed, life circumstances are so influential on this art. Is one period of life better for creative writing than another? Or is it just different? Also, there's some useful thinking to do around what patterns of behaviour we initiate to get pieces of writing finished or if there are several dimensions of involvement here, with us adopting certain ways of setting projects in motion, of keeping them going, and of concluding them. Because we're dealing with the physical and the psychological, as well as all the interpretative and responsive and emotive contexts of creating an art form, it makes perfect sense that we'll struggle to come to general conclusions about creative writing habitats. However, a few very interesting things emerge in the writers' comments.

'Anywhere' seems far more popular with creative writers here than might be expected! Perhaps no need to mention that in the making of some art forms 'anywhere' would not often be an option; many art forms require specific locations or specific equipment. The portability and flexibility of creative writing is not unique, but it is comparatively distinctive; and this also reflects on the ways in which information or facts are potentially used in creative writing. Where we find this information and how we use these facts is reflected in our writerly habitats, whether we adopt them or adapt them, whether they are long-term domestic spaces or places chosen to complete a project. If the impact of our chronological place in life and the portability of the writing arts are considerable influences on creative writing, we could add to these the role of the fortuitous or even what some might call the 'haphazard'. For every writer who makes a note on the role of discipline and of having their own space, there are probably an equal number of writers who will mention taking the chance to make notes on the back of an envelope or fitting in some creative writing at the end of a long day of doing something else.

Exercise

Imagine creative writing involves some kind of studio, some facility, containing equipment, and having certain operating hours. What would this look like for you? There is method in this question – the aim of it is to get us thinking about the physical and temporal attributes that contribute to creative writing. Let's entitle this exercise: 'The creative writing Studio' (suggested word length for this exercise: 1000 words).

Reflection

Have you ever counted how much you write – in lines or pages or words? If so, what was the result? Did it assist in setting goals or establishing a pattern of composition? If you've not tried this, would you like to try it as an experiment? It is worthwhile considering how we move from beginning a piece of writing to completing it, if only to locate those things that appear to constitute 'beginning', those that are essentially 'continuing' and those that are about 'finishing'. Do you work differently, at a different pace, in different ways, at each of these stages? Do you do everything in the same space, around the same times? Or does place and time change during your writing?

What things do you feel enhance your creative writing and what things challenge your ability to undertake it? Is this mostly to do with time? Does your writing gain in other ways, if you lose in time-terms?

9
Knowledge: Subjects and Themes

In writing about a variety of subjects and themes you've had to learn about various things. Is there any particular subject, or activity, you didn't imagine you'd ever know something about, that you do know about, because of your creative writing life?

This chapter can most productively be read in conjunction with the chapter that follows: the two chapters explore similar themes, but from alternate angles. Creative writing is an art, and it is a form of human communication. It is likewise a site of human knowledge and offers an exchange of knowledge between writers and their readers or audiences.

Discussions of certain aspects of Epistemology (the area of the field of Philosophy that deals with types and approaches to knowledge) underpin much that is in this book; after all, it is impossible to ask questions without requesting that someone share their knowledge. Every query assumes a form of an answer – even if the answer is incomplete at this point in our history.

In undertaking their work, all creative writers gain knowledge not only about creative writing but about the subjects and themes they write. The more difficult aspect of this concerns the identity, value and importance of this knowledge. What kind of knowledge is it that creative writers explore and develop and how might it be important? Assuming this knowledge has some value, how do we compare its value with that associated with other kinds of knowledge? How do we use this knowledge?

Logic suggests that while the creative writer writing about a hospital might come to know a great deal about healthcare it is far wiser to place our trust in a physician than a short story writer if we're seeking medical care! And yet, *something* is being discovered by that short story writer. What is it? Some kind of knowledge is being offered by you as a writer to the reader, and this knowledge is not inconsequential. But what kind of knowledge is this?

The field of Epistemology is a huge field of discussion and debate and, even though *Inside Creative Writing* has questions and answers at its core, solving wider epistemological issues is beyond this book's scope. That said, it is possible to speculate here on some of the relevant aspects for creative writing and creative writers.

Creative writing knowledge is strongly 'situational' – that is, it relates to the situation established in a particular work of creative writing, and it is initiated by the writer to bolster and support an individual kind of truth-making. Knowledge in creative writing is most often partial and it is most often applied – that is, creative writers seek out knowledge as far as is necessary to complete their works.

Though a creative writer might be stimulated to find out more, might even become personally enlivened by a subject or theme and keep learning about it beyond their poem or story or script, the essential element is that the knowledge they convey in their work (or works) came about because it was *required* to complete the work at hand, not because they sought it out more broadly.

As noted in the previous chapter, creative writing can involve knowledge recognisable to those in other fields – in the humanities, the natural sciences or the social sciences. While the role of the imagination might appear more prevalent, creative writing knowledge frequently arrives via observations highly filtered through layers of our personal interpretation and response. Such a degree of personalising by writers, and the often declared role of the writer's imagination, can mean writers' discoveries fail to conform to the methodologies and measurability found in other fields. However, it would be wrong to assume that this confirms a clear epistemological hierarchy – with 'hard' science knowledge at the top and 'soft' arts knowledge somewhere further down.

What creative writing knowledge involves is a kind of *setting up of a hypothesis* that the writer tests via the experiment of creating a work. This experiment might not aim for an entirely conclusive result. Rather, it could point to styles of understanding, offer possibilities of interpretation, or make connections between what the writer individually believes and what a range of others might believe. One key human value in this is that it draws out from others (that is, readers, audiences) something of their own investigations, it empowers them further by showing an example. Knowledge and understanding are exchanged, compared, even potentially grouped together in some fashion so, for example, a reader discovering a similar thread of understanding in the works of several creative could conclude that this knowledge is focal to a community and is widely agreed. This is *shared knowledge*. But, the primary modes of knowledge exchange here remain *individual*.

This is the most powerful human context of knowledge in creative writing. That is, that works of creative writing initiate, develop and support open and one-to-one exchange between human beings. In this communication agreements about what constitutes 'justified true belief',[1] come about. Creative writers are not often saying something along the lines of: 'I have tested all possible versions of what I believe and have found it supported by this testing. Here is my piece of creative writing and it arrives on the back of this testing.' Far more commonly creative writers are saying: 'I have learnt some things, and I perceive them to be correct. These things informed my understanding as I made this work of creative writing.'

In the realm of knowledge, and the exploration of knowledge, in and through creative writing, we certainly can call all this 'the big picture'! Variations on this picture include as many versions of creative writing subject, theme, genre and form as is imaginable. This is vast, perhaps even infinite. The smaller, but pragmatically significant, picture might seem mundane in comparison but, in fact, is just as remarkable. When a writer incorporates knowledge from other fields into their work, they try to avoid mistakes (unless made purposely for reasons of art, plot, character, voice and so forth). This avoiding of mistakes is not just a matter of professionalism, nor is it only about ensuring readers don't question the surface characteristics of a story or image. My suggestion is that creative writers endeavour to avoid factual mistakes and anachronisms because this contributes to the *justified true belief* contained in their finished works.

This is not to make a claim for the universality of knowledge in a work of creative writing. And the suggestion here is not that creative writing produces the same type or form of knowledge that can be found in the natural sciences, the social sciences or the humanities, even if it draws from those fields for a range of reasons. But it is asking us to acknowledge that as creative writers we learn things and we perceive things, and we incorporate this knowledge into the making of our works, and exchange this knowledge with their readers or audiences.

Sometimes this knowledge might be descriptive, suggestive and exploratory, sometimes it might be overtly factual (for example, in the use of historical dates), sometimes it might be concerned with the ways and means of accomplishing something. While this knowledge might be situational – that is developed because the writer is writing a particular work – and while it might be partial – that is, the writer writing about a hospital might not be a trained physician – this knowledge nevertheless has a purpose and an application. It also has substantial value.

* * *

Iain Banks

There are a few things I know a little more about now, thanks to doing research, that I wouldn't have expected to know so much about, but then I try to do as little research as I can because I am terribly lazy, so it's still not much really.

Charles Baxter

I had to learn something about theoretical physics and American Sign Language for *First Light*, about toxic waste for *Shadow Play*, and lately I've been learning about bomb-making. Bombs seem to be contemporary signifiers, if I could put it that way.

Andy Brown

My new book of poems, *Goose Music* – half the poems are written by me, half by John Burnside – contains 3 sequenced poems about mermaids. That subject matter was a complete surprise. I mean, 'I have heard the mermaids singing each to each, but did not think that they would sing to me'! The first mermaid poem is a sonnet about the merman who was captured and imprisoned in Orford Castle, in Suffolk in the Middle Ages. My in-laws live in Orford, and the subject simply presented itself to me on a visit one day. The second poem is about my brother-in-law, who *is* a merman. Well, he's a scuba diver, but that's close enough. Poetic license. On two occasions when he went scuba diving, the world changed whilst he was down there: the first was the occasion of Princess Diana's death; the second was on 9/11. My poem explores his sub-aqua world, but also asks what more world-changing news might arise the next time he goes diving. This gave me my link to the third poem, a long ballad about mermaids, which places the Gulf Wars in the English Channel, and brings those conflicts closer to home through a mermaid narrative. I researched myths about mermaids, nereids, sirens and selkies, and collaged a composite ballad that mixes these myths and legends. I never imagined I'd do anything of the sort.

I've also, in the past, researched varieties of Devon apples – with a particular interest in their wonderful names – Slack-ma-Girdle, Sops in Wine, Oaken Pin, Morgan Sweet, and many others – and have used those in poems and in prose fiction. Most of Devon's original orchards have now been grubbed up and lost, and so the varieties are lost too, along with the grounded practices of working the land in that manner. Writing the names of the apples into poems and stories is an act of ecological and cultural preservation; of conservation. I also write obsessively about birds and, as well as using the names, habits and habitats of birds, I've researched subjects concerning birds as diverse as mythologies and urban myths, as well as the lives of great bird artists such as John James Audubon.

More recently, my research has taken me into some theoretical arenas that have been a great source of surprise and intellectual stimulation for me. I'm particularly interested in Critical Realism, which is a theory of science that begins with ontology – how things *might be* – rather than beginning with epistemology (knowledge). One important facet of Critical Realism is Emergence. Emergence Theory describes how we build complex systems from very simple units. Ant colonies, bird flocks, the Internet, and cities are all examples of emergent systems: the individuals within the system don't know what everyone else is doing, but beautifully complex, unified patterns of behaviour emerge across the system as a whole. Poems too are emergent entities, as are poetic forms and poetic traditions. Researching these things I've also become engrossed by Externalism – the idea that our consciousness isn't simply something that happens *inside* our heads, rather that it also takes place *out there in the world*: the world is our consciousness, and the flow is two-way. Both Emergence and Externalism are extremely valuable ways of thinking for Ecopoetry, because they break down dualistic, mind-centred ways of thinking about the world, beginning instead with the things of the world themselves. They are philosophies of *being*, rather than philosophies of knowledge.

Maggie Butt

Lots. As a journalist and particularly as a TV documentary writer, I've become a short term world-expert on a variety of subjects – the history of shipbuilding, dowsing, self-build housing, pacifism. As a prose fiction writer I've interviewed people and read up on a wide range of things from Valium abuse to the Justice for Fathers campaign.

As a poet, I suppose I mainly draw on my existing knowledge, plus odd facts gleaned from Radio 4 or newspapers, or novels. I might follow up with some more research – about Kamikaze pilots, the invention of X-Rays, Canadian war brides, lipstick fashions in the Second World War, Hijabi women, environmental movements... Anything is fair game and everything is interesting. The writer is a kind of recycling centre, bringing together information and insight and memory and observation, and hopefully creating something new from it all.

Jack Epps Jr.

I believe in research. TOP GUN was a heavily researched film. I have my private pilot's license, and that sort of helped, but the difference between a private pilot and a Navy pilot is huge. I don't believe in faking a subject. I think one of the reasons TOP GUN was so successful is that I did about 45 hours of interviews, and then had them transcribed. I took their stories and wove them together. So, basically, the entire film, with a lot of Hollywood embellishment, is a series of true stories. These events really happened to pilots, so the film is based on reality. We add the creative stories.

I can't write something I don't have a feeling for. A small tiny love story would be difficult for me. I am a big movie guy. My instincts are for the wide screen. I write with the giant screen in mind. When I go see a film, I go to the biggest screen in Los Angeles and watch it. This is what movies are to me. Bigger than life stories.

But I don't like to lie on screen and make up a lot of fiction. I write from my own emotions, and I do research so that I understand the heart of the characters and the story. Research gives you story. It gives you truth. It gives the screenplay a solid foundation to work from. I was talking recently with James L. Brooks about TERMS OF ENDEARMENT and the Jack Nicholson character. A key character to that film. Nicholson's character, the astronaut, was not in Larry McMurtry's original novel. Jim found the character by doing extensive research in Houston where the story was set. It's hard to imagine that film without the Nicholson character. Jim learned something by spending six months in Houston.

Research gives a writer stories. People love to talk about themselves, and they tell stories. Get people talking, and they will give you a ton of material. The hard part is finding the narrative thread, taking all those little pieces and making them into one coherent story.

Nadine Gordimer

Writing is exploration, for me. I am always coming upon varieties of experience, human responses, capacities, before me, opening up new thoughts, demanding understanding.

Kate Grenville

The book I've just finished is about an astronomer/mathematician in the late eighteenth century. I am spectacularly bad at that kind of thinking – bad at arithmetic, not good at the kind of mental gymnastics necessary to understand the ecliptic or precession let alone calculus and the lunar distance method of determining longitude. I wouldn't say I have a handle on them now, but engaging with them – and reading books by and about mathematicians – has been an enrichment of my interior life. I'm in awe of the creativity of mathematics.

Nessa O'Mahony

The whole issue of emigration and Diaspora is something that I hadn't given any thought to before I began a writing project that involved telling the story of a nineteenth-century Irish woman who emigrated to Australia in the 1850s. I was living in Wales at the time, so felt something of an emigrant myself, and so was more and more drawn to exploring how living elsewhere impacts on a writer. As I write this, I'm half way through a residency at University College Dublin on the theme of Diaspora so I've had a further opportunity to explore this and am fascinated by how different writers and artists have reacted differently to living away from home, or else having a first- or second-generation relationship with another country.

Ruth Padel

Yes – lots – biology especially. I was never good at science at school.

Robert Pinsky

I lack the scholarly qualities of thoroughness and precision, but I am an active, busy kind of jackdaw. When I meet a roofer or a designer of mutual funds, it's second nature for me to learn a bit about roofing or the design of investment instruments. One risks trying for intelligent questions, maybe even showing off a gem of acquired baloney or two.

Possibly, compared to some poets I am a bit like the fiction writer doing research. But in my own sporadic, somewhat random manner: having fun in the wrong part of the library, or the adjacent volume of the encyclopaedia.

So I've picked up a little about the tools and materials: the nature of paper, the principles of the digital computer, the parts of a book. In such areas, I tend to have a bit of information, some arcane vocabulary, and a few near-misses as to correctness. Pastern, fetlock, ham string, mechlin, balance pawl, parting-bead, etc. The galvanized flashing around the chimney, the use of the froe, similar to cost-averaging or indexing.

Philip Pullman

I suppose there is. If I make an effort I can remember what I found out about balloons and early Arctic exploring, for instance. But I've forgotten most of that now. The point is that I know where the information is if I need it again. The other point I'd make about that kind of thing is that you don't have to get everything pin-point accurate. The function of 'research' is to enable you, not to get all the facts about – for example – the mechanics of Victorian ballooning dead right, but to make up what you *don't* know in a way that looks convincing. I'm a great believer in *the explanation that satisfies at the time*. You know Hitchcock's McGuffin, the thing that's unimportant in itself (the diamond necklace, the secret plans) but which sets off the plot? I think *the explanation that satisfies at the time* deserves a name as well. I call it the McKipper. 'Why does the balloonist have to fly so low, when he has enough gas to fly higher?' 'Because the Stacy-Pattison valve tends to stick at these low temperatures.' 'Oh, right! I understand now.' That's a McKipper.

Tom Shapcott

Well, I have become a sort of expert on late 19th Hungary; and on the ballet world of Vaslav Nijinsky. This would never have come about had I not researched for the novel WHITE STAG OF EXILE. Similarly I researched the Siege of Leningrad for THE SEARCH FOR GALINA. In poetry I undertook research on the timber Australian Red Cedar (Toona Australia). Other poems came from incidental reading (Macadamia Nuts; the colonial Governor Macquarie, Commandant Logan etc etc). A friend, Eva Sallis, has learned Russian for her new novel; Roger Macdonald learned to ride a horse and to fly for his second novel.

William Tremblay

Is there any subject or activity you didn't imagine you'd ever know about that you learned because of writing?

Yes. I come from Massachusetts but I've lived in northern Colorado for 35 years. One sunny January 1990 morning I looked up at the snowy mountains and the beauty of the mountains suddenly ava-lanched into me. I wanted to know what Colorado was like 150 years ago. I read *The History of Larimer County* [1905] by Ansel Watrous and found that he had written to Antoine Janis, a mountain man who married Red Cloud's sister, First Elk Woman, and who was the first white man to receive 160 acres through the Homestead Act in 1864. Watrous had written to him at Pine Ridge asking for 'all the particu-lars' as to the founding of LaPorte, Colorado, and Janis replied that his health was such he could not undertake to tell the tale. So, I saw a 'what if' situation, and I stepped into it, deciding to write an apocry-phal account of Janis's life in the form of a series of letters. In so doing I learned a lot of things about the mountain trails of Colorado, about the beaver trade, about the mountain men, their lore, their skills, their knowledge, their sense of humour ['tall tales'], their knowledge of the Native American tribes, their languages, religions, customs, relations with other tribes, the scope of their nomadic wanderings over the western landscapes, the history of the axe in North America, family life, hunting buffalo, many trips to Fort Laramie, Wyoming. A matter of three years. What a ride! Now I am a volunteer for the United States Forest Service, working on the trail crew, educating the public about the wilderness.

Xu Xi

The Flying Tigers. Interest began when I made the father of one of my characters a pilot, and I was working at Federal Express at the time which had purchased, a few years earlier, the cargo airline Flying Tigers, which grew out of the WWII Tigers fighter pilots. I vaguely knew something about the original Tigers but not a whole lot. My publisher then who tends to know interesting people said he knew an old Tigers guy in Guangzhou, one of the Chinese guys who flew with CAT (China Air Transport), and would I like to meet him so I said why not. From that the research began and in the next book, I carried through the same character who now had a half sister who shared the same Flying Tigers father so I began reading a little more about the Tigers. And then after that book was done the half sister who was one of 4 characters in the previous book became the protagonist of the next book (the one coming out this fall) and the Tigers research meant reading yet more books, including this gorgeous novel by

James Salter (*The Hunters*) which has a fighter pilot as a protagonist. I don't come out of a military background at all, but I now know more than I ever expected to know about purple hearts, the Tigers, fighter pilots, silver stars, 'kills', Claire Chennault (the Tigers founder), the author of *The Little Prince* (Saint Exupery was a fighter pilot), and different makes of aircraft (the Cessna is particularly elegant). I mean I worked for an airline in my twenties and loved travel etc. but didn't know much about pilots etc., just load factor and frequent flyer programs, because that was what the business end cared about.

Edvard Munch. From a girlfriend who first brought me to the MOMA and stood me in front of a Munch painting because, she said, she thought I might like his work, I have spent years chasing down the man and his art and life. I did use a Munch painting in one of my short stories, and I have at this point done more research on him than I have actually used in a creative piece – I did start a novella with his work as a central metaphor (metaphor for what I still haven't quite defined). I spent one summer in Norway where I travelled to various places he lived as well as haunted the Munch Museum (once I discovered that the bulk of his work is housed in Oslo and not in museums elsewhere I knew I had to go to Norway). I've made two other trips to Norway as well, and the last time, I got into the house where he died. As a result of all this hoofing around Nordic museums, I discovered a minor Danish painter Henry Brokman whose work I've chased down (he lived mostly in Sorrento) with the idea that his paintings might feature in another novella (do you detect a similar strain here) but this two-novella book keeps getting postponed in favour of more research and other novels that want to be written first.

Penile Agenesis. For a character in a long story that has since been published in serial form. Don't even know how that got started but once it did I read what I could get my hands on and haunted on line sites for those with the condition. All this ended once I finished the story.

The American Songbook. Lyrics, music, composers, lyricists, jazz and other versions of specific tunes, the origins of jazz standards from the songbook (e.g.: Isn't it Romantic – I think I own every version ever recorded; Vernon Duke who wrote 'Autumn in New York' among other tunes; Hoagy Carmichael who sings better than he plays piano but who composed some amazing tunes, Hart who was the lyricist Rodgers should not have given up for Hammerstein even though he made a bigger name for himself with the latter because collaboration with the former gave him the better songs). I've always loved music and play piano and was married to a jazz musician for years and lived the jazz life, but the amount of extra research I've done into the American Songbook surprised even me. It was for a character who sings, but then I kept going way beyond what was needed for the novel (unlike previous musical research into, e.g.: Paganini's Violin Concerto in D which ended when I finished that novel).

There are other subjects I learned for things I wrote, but these four stand out because they were unusual in their intensity.

* * *

Because creative writing is never involves a fixed process, how much we need to know to complete any work of creative writing, what we need to know, can be a vexed question. By 'never fixed' I mean that the artistic results that emerge from creative writing have a degree of fixity as material objects but the making of them is all about our human actions, and the completion of them often involves an element of stopping rather than truly 'finishing'. As objects then, of course, they are then open to the reading and interpreting of readers or audiences. So to an extent even then they continue to remain in motion.

What I was hoping in this chapter was that the writers in *Inside Creative Writing* would indicate their surprising discovery moments – those points where they realised that they had learnt something, perhaps through situational necessity, that they never thought they might know, that might not even have been on their personal radars before commencing some writing. The writers have noted this, and it's astounding to read of such a range of new things learnt among a relatively small selection of creative writers.

William Tremblay, for example, tells the story of wanting 'to know what Colorado was like 150 years ago'. Xu Xi, alternatively, tells the story of 'The Flying Tigers'. Tom Shapcott became a 'sort of expert on late nineteenth century Hungary; and on the ballet world of Vaslav Nijinsky'. Iain Banks has learnt 'something about theoretical physics and American Sign', 'toxic waste' and 'bomb-making'. And for Nadine Gordimer, quite simply, 'writing is exploration'.

All this makes you wonder, what volume and extent of knowledge would we find if we were to poll *all* the creative writers in the world? It's a miraculous thought – imagining all those who engaged in creative writing and what they have discovered in the undertaking of their creative writing!

What dawns also is the awareness that creative writing is indeed about exploration, and that creative writing involves a certain sense of human wonder. Creative writers research, in every sense of that word; they seek out facts, but also they seek to interpret. There is a natural openness about this because how this new knowledge is used, how it is incorporated into a work of creative writing and how far the writer explores what can be called the 'situational necessity' of finding things out is not part of a shared code between writers.

Indeed, the methods of using and developing knowledge through creative writing are not codified at all; expectations about them are not regularly discussed, not even among writers themselves. We rarely hear creative writers commenting that they are adhering to some particular theoretical position in their research and/or their general use of new information. Dare I say, there is also a degree of deference about this – while we creative writers might proudly say that we know something about a field or idea or concept or, conceivably, an emotion or feeling, we will also often make clear that we don't consider ourselves experts.

This chapter and the one that follows are intimately linked. Thinking on what kind of knowledge is used by creative writers, what kind we produce and what kind we exchange, draws us to consider how creative and critical understanding in this art form comes about. There is procedural or technical knowledge involved (that is, knowledge about the craft of creative writing) at the same time as knowledge of subjects and themes. Likewise, creative writers have to perceive some future, completed artistic object, in order to proceed. In other words, our making assumes something that eventually will be made. Actions and objects each display writerly knowledge, and the two interact – as we'll see in the chapter that follows. In all these things we witness a series of knowledge exchanges, a series that is as fascinating as it is integral to creative writing.

Exercise

An obvious exercise to explore is one involving your analysing of the types of knowledge that informed your undertaking of one particular piece of creative writing. In the interests of going a little further with this, can you now outline the knowledge you pursued and applied in terms of (a) culture or cultures (b) what might be called the 'visceral' elements (that is, knowledge connected with an impulse or with emotions rather than knowledge connected with the intellect) and (c) knowledge that, on discovery, substantially altered the course of your piece of creative writing? (suggested word length for this exercise, (a)–(c): total 1000 words).

Reflection

This chapter has focussed on knowing, on discovering things. But how many instances can you recall where the desire to find out initiated some creative writing? That is, have you already a list of instances where *not knowing* rather than knowing was integral to undertaking some creative writing?

Recalling to the earlier healthcare and physician example – how would you personally use the knowledge found in a work of creative writing? If it turned out this knowledge had limited utilitarian importance, would this matter? Were that the case, what other roles might this knowledge serve?

10
Writing Craft and Skills

Question 9 was my way of sliding into this more difficult question! I best admit that up-front. I'm interested in the idea of knowledge associated with creative writing. Obviously, some of this is concerned with what is sometimes called 'skills' or 'craft'. But this seems a narrow way of describing the knowledge creative writers use, knowledge they have, knowledge they acquire, or even knowledge they provide for others through their works. Dare I ask: have you any thoughts on this? I'm also interested in the question of how valuable this knowledge can be, or might be. But that might be asking too much!

The previous chapter largely left out a consideration of creative writing as a craft, as a skill-based activity. The main reason for doing this was to approach creative writing firstly as a holder of human knowledge, a container as well as a user of knowledge. Now let's turn to the craft.

A great many books have been written on the craft of writing. Many of these books are called 'how to books'. The broader context of writerly knowledge is often absent from these books. But neither these books nor their focus on craft is incorrect, even if that focus is somewhat narrow. We certainly can say that creative writing *is* a craft because it is a human activity involving a particular set of skills and it is a physical activity. However, our investigation doesn't stop here.

Actually, we might ask whether creative writing is both craft and art? So far I have opted for calling it both an art and a form of communication, but I have not used that word craft. This is entirely a prejudice on my part, and it now needs addressing. I have not so far called creative writing a craft because so often discussions of creative writing have stopped at questions of 'how to' and failed to engage with it as human practice involving far more than skills, combining our creative and our critical understanding, both being partially displayed in completed works of creative writing.

I prefaced my Question 10 by telling the writers that I had pre-empted the examination anyway, though I was aware that I was taking us into ever more difficult territory. A lot of what has been researched about creative writing has been premised on the notion that completed works – e.g. novels, poems, scripts – hold the key clues, and whatever is found in these works will unearth these key aspects of the writers' art or craft. This is said to be the case, even if professional critical trends have veered away from suggesting that meaning might be firmly located only in these texts or, indeed, the 'author' discovered in them.

This is a difficult territory because if we accept that criticism of completed works does not reach far enough towards the *actual* activities of creative writing to unearth all we might wish to discover about it, then what do we do? If we cannot find out more by critically examining those completed works, where then do we look for our answers? If we have not discussed creative writing with the vast majority of creative writers (that is, with those writers whose finished works are not widely known to us, because these are indeed the creative writers who make up most of the world's population of creative writers), what then? If we have not seen the finished works, the drafts, the notes, all manner of writing evidence form these, the majority of the world's creative writers, how do we proceed to understand creative writing?

Perhaps most importantly we can improve our understanding by not separating a consideration of *knowledge* in creative writing from a consideration of *skills* in creative writing, and by not dealing with end *results* separately from the actual, ongoing activities of *doing* creative writing.

Question 9 and Question 10 here are therefore not separated along the lines of 'theory' versus 'practice', or 'activities' versus 'criticism' or 'skills' versus 'knowledge'. But the issue remains whether creative writing can be both art and a craft. As it turns out, this issue goes beyond our interest in creative writing. David Revere McFadden, Chief Curator and Vice President, Museum of Arts & Design, New York, says this:

> Craft, art, and design are words heavily laden with cultural baggage. For me, they all connote the profound engagement with materials and process that is central to creativity. Through this engagement form, function, and meaning are made tangible. It is time to move beyond the limitations of terminologies that fragment and separate our appreciation of creative actions, and consider the 'behaviours of making' that practitioners share.[1]

Behaviours of making is an extremely useful way of describing what occurs in creative writing. The general definition of behaviour is a *response in context*, and much of what we do in creative writing is exactly that: a response in context. Considering behaviours of making gives us a clue to approaching knowledge and skill in creative writing, even if we have to remind ourselves that our behaviour also incorporates critical engagement, is often multi-layered (that is, it involves levels of mental processing as well as physical activity), and that these behaviours produce objects as results – that is, works of creative writing, complete, incomplete, partial, personal or public.

So – is creative writing art *or* craft, art *and* a craft? David Revere McFadden is right that these terms are laden with cultural baggage and don't get us any closer to creative writing itself. However, to take a position: art is often defined as including craft or crafting and that could well be the best way to consider it. Art is the inclusive term. Craft is an element of it. Craft is a description of the skill-based activities in this art of creative writing.

* * *

Iain Banks

I think one can write very well without having a great spread of knowledge, and there are styles of writing where you just keep everything very vague and get away with knowing very little about subjects a reader might expect you would know rather a lot about, but then that depends on who you're writing for, for one thing. Generally you need to know a fair bit about what you're writing about, but then as a lot of stories are about people, families, relationships and such playground basics as love, hate, jealousy, promises, betrayals and so on, pretty much everybody already has that knowledge inbuilt anyway, before they even get to secondary school, let alone a university creative writing course. Perhaps the greatest knowledge a writer can have apart from that is that which comes from having read a lot (and preferably – arguably – from having read a lot of what is generally termed serious or quality literature). Oh, and knowing yourself, having a degree of self-honesty; that helps too.

Charles Baxter

This is a tricky question, and one that probably separates British and American writers. American culture has always been pragmatic, at least from the early nineteenth century; there is a feeling in this culture that you can learn how to do anything, often from how-to books. Our only real contribution to philosophy has been the philosophy of Pragmatism. The British have often looked upon American practicality with bemused wonder. They know, after all, that not everyone can learn how to do just anything. American culture is flooded with books about how to write fiction, how to go about doing it. We have spawned a culture of creative writing, and sometimes it seems that we have more writers than readers, and that 'creative writing' in this country is a gigantic Ponzi scheme. There is a kind of knowledge that can be acquired about writing, but much of it is intuitive and cannot be learned solely from books. Henry James once said that there are rules for writing, but there are a million of them, and many of them can be used only once.

Andy Brown

Well, as I said above, I'm more interested in thinking about *being* than I am in *knowledge*, so I think the question comes at things from the wrong way round. To begin with questions of *knowledge* puts the cart before the horse. *Being* comes before *knowledge* in both time and logic. If we ask 'What can we know?' the rather tired postmodern idea that we can't know anything for sure comes crashing in. We end up swilling around in the infinite regress of aesthetic and moral relativism. If, instead, we ask questions about being; about the nature of things – 'How might things be in order for us to know anything about them?' – then we have something to build on, for things certainly *are*. The writer must begin with those things; everything else is intangible abstraction.

I'm afraid I also have a problem with the idea that 'skill' and 'craft' is a 'narrow' way of thinking about writing. Why is it 'narrow' to technically and imaginatively excel at the thing that you do; that's a lifetime's endeavour isn't it?

These are both preambles to the main point I want to make, however, which is to return us to *readers*. It's of very little interest to me to think about the knowledge that any given writer may acquire for themselves because, without a reader, *writer you are nothing*. The knowledge is *all* to do with the reader. Yes, it might make the writer more 'interesting', because of the knowledge they've acquired but, ultimately, so what? That kind of knowledge is egocentric, and can only make a difference if the writer is also their only reader. Real knowledge is cultural, emergent and outlives any given individual. Until someone picks up the book, listens to the radio play, watches the film, goes to the theatre or poetry reading, that knowledge sits inert on the page. We go to writers to be changed; the writer is merely the agent of that change. The writer taps into the world through language and presents it to readers – what 'knowledge' comes out of that contract is then all to do with readers. Writers live and writers die; we come and go and, if we are lucky, our words may live on. What any given writer 'knows' about words, or about the world, is only a very small part of this much bigger picture. That's what I'm interested in.

Maggie Butt

The easier part of this is about skills or craft, which I continue to learn by reading others and analysing how they've done something, then doing it badly myself, then doing it better, and of course by teaching it and giving feedback to other people about what works and what doesn't, and trying to recognise those failings in my own work.

But skills knowledge on its own wouldn't produce a satisfying work. It has to combine with the factual knowledge you asked about earlier, and with tacit knowledge, with imaginative intuitions and insights which are personal to the writer.

These knowledges are cake ingredients which need to be combined in the right quantities, but which won't work without the chemical magic of the raising agents and the heat. It's the drawing together of all those things which can bring the surprises and the excitement. And – like baking – some cakes turn out better than others!

The most mysterious knowledge is that which occasionally emerges in the act of writing, when you find you have written something which you didn't know you knew...

Jack Epps Jr.

I think this goes back to what I was saying earlier. I think it's more important for a writer to develop instincts than knowledge. There is a cottage industry that has sprung up in the last few years around how to write screenplays. The sorry fact is that almost all of those books are written by people who have never written a screenplay, or if they have, it has never been produced. What do they know about the process?

I think writing, like everything, has a learning curve. I know that I read a ton of screenplays, watched every movie I could get my hands on, and tried to figure out how it worked. I am very analytical so I did scene by scene breakdowns of movies I admired and formed my own theories. I'm self-educated in how to write. Most successful writers are self-taught.

I was an English major in college and read novels endlessly. It was great training. The basic laws of literature and theatre work for screenplays too. Screenplays are limited by time – 2 hours. A novel takes you *inside* the character, while in a screenplay you watch *what happens to* the character in the moment. I'm not a big believer in flashbacks. Movies for me are here and now. They are immediate. I don't do a lot of back stories because I want to know what is happening to the character now. Why now? And what does it mean to this person at this time? Movies are immediate. Characters deal with their problems now.

That being said, I do believe a writer can learn the craft. I am the Chair of the Writing Division at the School of Cinematic Arts at the University of Southern California. We teach craft and a good competent writer can learn how to write solid journeyman screenplays.

I can't teach talent, but I can nurture talent, and I can help a young writer develop instincts. A talented writer can learn how to be more effective. I also am concerned about honing instincts. Expose the young writer to the tools and elements of screenwriting, and then encourage them to trust themselves.

But you can't learn to write by reading about it, you have to write, write, write. You have good days and you have bad days. More bad days than good days until you learn enough so that your bad days are actually pretty good.

What's important to know is once again a William Goldman quote: 'nobody knows anything.' There is no one way. Each writer has their own voice, perspective, point of view, tone, instinct and approach to the material. Ultimately, these need be the guiding principles the writer must listen to. I abhor any sort of approach that says on page 30 you must do this, and on page 60 you must do this. Bullshit. Not true. A bunch of malarkey. You tell a good story one page at a time. If you can't hold the reader, then you're not doing it right.

It all comes down to telling a good story on paper. It doesn't matter when it happens, as long as I want to turn the next page to find out what happens next. And if I'm not emotionally invested in the main character, then I don't care about what happens to them in the end.

Nadine Gordimer

If you want to understand Napoleon's retreat from Moscow, what it meant to the Russians and what it meant to his soldiers, to soldiers on both sides, you have to read Tolstoy, not a history book.

Kate Grenville

The most irrelevant knowledge seems the most useful for a creative writer – the bits and pieces you have in your head that you might not have known were there and might not have valued.

In terms of writerly knowledge, I'm very glad I studied all those old writers as part of my BA degree – Chaucer, Wyatt, Sir Thomas Browne, Montaigne. I think what they taught me is that any kind of writing can engage the reader, and so as a writer you can take more risks and be bolder than you might think.

At the later stages of writing (I mean after about draft 10 or 12) it's useful to be able to give names and functions to the marks on the page – to be able to think about point of view and paragraphing etc – just because you then can see that you have a choice. You've written it in one point of view, for example, but if you know a little about the idea of point of view you realise you have other choices – there isn't just one chisel in the toolkit but a whole roll of them for different purposes. But I also think you can get bogged down in technicalities, and definitely that if you start thinking about them too early the writing goes dead.

Nessa O'Mahony

There's a lengthy tradition of writers sharing knowledge with each other; this has become more formalised in recent years through the development of creative writing programmes at second and third level, but the master apprentice relationship has always been there, I think. I sense you are suggesting something wider here, though, about the skills that creative writers learn and use and whether they could be applied more widely? I've facilitated creative writing workshops for people who have been out of work as a result of disability and who are trying to re-skill and build confidence. I've found that creative writing can boost people's confidence enormously because they discover a skill they didn't know they had, and have fun making that discovery.

Ruth Padel

Writers get off on different things. Because I was trained as an academic, or because of something in my genes, I do sometimes find a poem gets going imaginatively by knowledge of different sorts. Then I have to follow where it leads. But it has to be absorbed into the muscle of the poem – a poem is not a machine for handing knowledge over.

Robert Pinsky

Creative writing students must read, read, read, read, read – and they must read the way a cook eats or a filmmaker watches movies. What you must know, in order to know your art, is as great a range of your art as possible. That includes historical range and geographical range and cultural range. If all you know is your contemporaries, or the equivalent of the gang at the office, or the crowd that hangs about on the high road or in the plaza, you are not likely to do much that is very fresh or original.

If you are serious, study the range. And decide what you think is magnificent.

Every aspiring writer should keep an ever-expanding personal day-book or anthology: specific examples, that you have copied out long-hand or typed (which means memorizing it a few words at a time, in order to write or type it) or what you consider magnificent writing. If you have only a dozen pages, or if everything is from one time period or one culture...then your talent is undernourished. You must feed it properly, with knowledge.

Knowledge of the art: writerly knowledge, which is not always what professional scholars in universities understand or honour.

Learn your instrument, and learn what has been done with it.

And it can't be anyone else's 'curriculum' or 'canon'. It's ok to listen to teachers, but ultimately your guide is your own sense of what is magnificent. That is your compass, internal in reading as in writing.

Philip Pullman

I'm not quite sure what you mean by this, other than the sort of things you can find in any woodworking magazine under the title 'Tip of the month', in which someone points out that you can make a very handy jig for your bandsaw with a piece of MDF and two bot-tle tops. There are narrative things I've discovered (like the McKipper above) [previous chapter], and I suppose if I had nothing else to do I could write them down in a book and persuade someone to publish them, but it seems more fun to put them into practice.

Tom Shapcott

All knowledge is useful; it is what distinguishes us. With some of the knowledge gained, I have been able to be a sort of encyclo-paedia to others, as well as my own resourced-bank for my own (future) writing. In other words, I have been able to dine out on all that; and many times. This applies to others I know, and not only writers. As for disseminating such knowledge: my poem/perform-ance-piece on Macadamia nuts has been broadcast on the ABC radio science show, and also to the Annual Meeting of the Australian Professional Macadamia Nut Association.

William Tremblay

Is it all a matter of techniques of putting the words down or does creative writing involve other kinds of skills and knowledge?

The 'other' skills and knowledge I think of as 'inner work'. It may be more important than a mastery of form and technique. But it is elu-sive, difficult, highly individualized, and probably inimitable. Some use meditation; some use dialectics; some use an attitude of continu-ous irony. The range is very wide.

As one looks at an image or a line of poetry like 'Because I could not stop for death' or 'Something there is that does not love a wall' one hears the onset of discourse, an announcement of subject and theme. The question is, How is it going to develop? Among the stra-tegic questions we may include: Is it going to operate by additive detail? Antithesis? Erasure? Subtraction? Assertion or assertorial light-ness? How is it going to work itself down the page? Will it introduce seemingly irrelevant facts? Will it telescope outwards to gain context? Or inward to microscopic universes? The processes involved enact the poet's way of processing his or her realities and may reflect his or her characteristic moves or gestures toward subject and theme. Some frame their poetic inner work around methods of interrogating one's environment and projecting desires. For the last 150 years the pressures of reality have been ambiguous, even contradictory; often discourse sorts through opposed half-truths.

Xu Xi

I have written a lot about Hong Kong – its people, the city, a little on the history, contemporary culture, various iconic characters, etc. – and if there is one piece of 'knowledge' that I feel is of value which my readers acquire, it is a view of Hong Kong that goes far beyond what the tourist association or martial arts movies provide. The craft side is actually less interesting to me except for teaching, as content does seem to me the reason we write.

* * *

It cannot help but strike us that learning creative writing involves more than skills but that *without* certain skills you simply cannot do it! That is stating the obvious, but less obvious queries then arise as to how we judge the level of our skills, as well as how others might judge our skills. The complications in this grow ever more intriguing, because we might then consider whether a creative writer with great skill always is always a great creative writer?

Patently this is not always the case. Therefore, we can't mean only the technical skills of writerly composition, we must also mean something else when we talk about creative writing 'skills'. This plural term suggests we can list a set of things that any one creative writer has learnt – so, Writer X is very good at composing the villanelle form, or Writer Y is an extremely capable creator of film characters. But this is skimming the surface of something, however accurate it might first appear. It isn't then the plural form that points us in the right direction to answer this question. 'Skill' (singular), meaning a proficiency, a facility for something – that is a better word.

Others have considered this relation between skill and knowledge. Writing in the *Journal of Higher Education*, Ference Marton says:

> An important problem is that cognitive skills are often regarded as being over and above knowledge. In actual fact, cognitive skills would seem to have more to do with the nature of knowledge and how it is handled by the individual. Thus cognitive skills are not, in our opinion, independent of knowledge. On the contrary, we see skills as aspects of knowledge.[2]

So, 'cognitive skills' (things like our perception, our reasoning, our judgement) are embedded in our knowledge. But cognitive skills only explain *some* element of the undertaking of creative writing. Cognition – reasoning, perception, the intellectual and factual – is most often contrasted with emotional intelligence, free will, our intuition. In any art we would not wish to reduce either the skill or the knowledge involved only to the cognitive, we'd also acknowledge these other elements.

If we return to the concept of 'behaviours of making' we gather something of what we need to go further with this, adding to this a consideration of the objects of our making that emerge before, during and after we have been undertaking some creative writing. Adding to this too the recognition that these behaviours, like all behaviours, refer to aspects of human stimulus and response, and that these behaviours are learnt – in essence, in creative writing we use tools (that is, words, sentences, a language) that are not known to us innately.

These behaviours incorporate the 'narrative things I've discovered' in Philip Pullman's case, and the development of 'instincts' mentioned by Jack Epps Jr. They relate to Kate Grenville's 'bits and pieces you have in your head that you might not have known were there and might not have valued'. And to Andy Brown asking questions 'about being; about the nature of things' and William Tremblay's 'inner work'. They are most certainly behaviours of making in the realm of Maggie Butt's 'cake ingredients which need to be combined in the right quantities, but which won't work without the chemical magic of the raising agents and the heat.'

What is not confirmed in this is that while we all must learn creative writing, while we all combine knowledge of subjects and themes with knowledge containing our degree of individual skill, we also draw on something that might be called our *disposition* – in other words, our character, our temperament or personality.

Does this mean, given that this character contains elements that are part of our individual being, that one creative writer might possess personal characteristics that potentially makes them a stronger writer, a better writer, than another. That one writer might, in this sense, be more talented than another. Yes, of course. As with any humans we creative writers are indeed a combination of *nature* and *nurture*.

Reflection

If skill is contained in knowledge and, as such, knowledge can be considered as such a container of skill can you list, say five elements of your physical crafting that are grounded in a broader sense of knowledge in the field of creative writing?

Exercise

Sometimes those in the field of Business Studies conduct what is called a SWOT analysis. *S*trengths, *W*eaknesses, *O*pportunities and *T*hreats. Creative writers are rarely averse to drawing information and ideas from any field of endeavour that can inform their work. Is there anything you might gain from a personal SWOT analysis of your knowledge/skill? Why not try one now? (suggested word length for this exercise: 100–150 words on each of the *S*trengths, *W*eaknesses, *O*pportunities and *T*hreats relating to *knowledge*, and then the *S*trengths, *W*eaknesses, *O*pportunities and *T*hreats relating to *skill*).

Reflection

Not an encouragement to ignorance, but perhaps an encouragement to question the role of the intellectual. That is, is there anything in or about creative writing that you would not want to *know*? In this case, by 'know' I mean have a logical reasoned certainty about.

11
Reading and Not Writing

Creative writers, generally, say they are keen readers. On the other hand, some have said that if they do jobs other than their writing, they prefer to do things that are at least a little (sometimes a lot) removed from creative writing. What's your writing–reading activity? Do you mostly read things connected with the main work you're undertaking at the time? Or do you read whatever you feel like reading, or have a more general reading preference? Do you do any things quite consciously not to be writing, or not to be thinking about writing?

Though this book is about writing, it is not necessarily that most writing will come to us as words to be read. It is more likely that for most of us written words, sentences, whole written volumes of words will arrive aurally as spoken text.

Similarly, though we read, most of what we read will not consist of works of creative writing. Even if we are avid readers of works of creative writing, it is more likely that other, somewhat more mundane reading matter – road signs, credit card bills, circulars, telephone company offers by text, supermarket fliers and any number of 'spam' emails – will provide the majority of our reading or, perhaps more accurately, our involuntary reading experiences.

When immersed in something, it is easy to come to believe that how our personal world works is how the world works in general. Creative writing is a widely enjoyed human activity. But, frankly, most people in the world don't do it regularly. Most people in the world don't connect their reading habitats with anything to do with doing some creative writing. Because forms of reading are commonly encountered, it is instructive to investigate whether creative writers have any characteristic reading strategies.

Because of how we occupy ourselves, we creative writers are probably the people most likely to concern themselves with who is consuming works of creative writing (though we must of course include the professional interests of publishers and those producing media, theatre and so forth in this category too). The writers in this book undertake creative writing as their profession, even if they might also do it for enjoyment. So, again, it could be instructive to investigate if professional writers, connected in some way with the activities of the creative industries (publishing and so forth), divide their reading between reading undertaken for work and reading undertaken for pleasure. Perhaps that division between 'reading for work' and 'reading for pleasure' doesn't matter, practically. Perhaps it is false altogether, because all reading is relevant to us personally, in some fashion; *all reading matters, in some way.*

Plainly, works of creative writing can be included in the realms of entertainment, leisure and fun as much as anywhere else. Certain genre, certain works, certain representations of contemporary cultural movements will become of interest to those in academia. Versions of the expression 'I've been reading for fun lately, not only for work' are not uncommon around universities and colleges. There are, it might be said, people we can most accurately call 'professional readers', as well as those we call professional creative writers.

When a particular work of literature, film or theatre becomes one of the mainstays of a period in professional, academic criticism, chances are that any number of professional readers will be concerning themselves with it. In the meantime, works of creative writing might be the mainstays of general, popular consumption. In some cases, these can be the same works as those of interest to academe. In many cases, they might be other works. There is no hard and fast rule about the division of interest here. Consumption of books, films, plays, digital texts and more, all returns us to questions of the role of specific interest groups and our purpose in producing these works. But the human impetus for reading is located prior to all this, it comes from something far more elementary in us.

As creatures, we humans *read* the weather, the seasons, the tides. By reading, in this instance, I mean 'attempt to comprehend'. We 'endeavour to get to know'. Reading is one of our primary human survival techniques, an essential activity for living. If this primal sort of reading is different to the reading of creative writing, then we need to consider how it is different because it surely involves so very much that is similar.

Comprehension, interpretation, seeking meaning, our consideration and analysis – all these familiar aspects of reading texts are also part of our *primal* reading. Human beings read faces, we read moods, we read situations and we read intentions. Our social needs determine this, and our success in life often strongly depends upon it. We read, by our nature, and by our application of attention to the world around us. It is obvious that we don't only read words. Far from it! We humans are readers of all kinds of creature movements and positions and even in the realm of textual reading we are readers of images, still images and moving images.

How we read, to what purposes we read, in what circumstances we read, and to what ends we read, is a good place to start to ponder our writerly relationships with reading. When we do this, we won't be able to completely abandon the baggage of cultural influence – nor, more specifically, the baggage concerned with hierarchies of cultural importance that determine what is considered 'good things to read' and what is considered 'bad things to read'.

There might indeed be merit in being guided by assessments of what constitutes excellence. Our engagement with examples of excellent works of creative writing no doubt guide us in pursuing excellence in our own creative work – whether we read these while we are writing, or we read these before or after we are writing. But, equally, if reading is a natural human trait, then our acts of reading go well beyond any single cultural notion of what is 'good' and we can conceive them as part of our wider engagement with living and writing.

*   *   *

Iain Banks

I don't read fiction when I'm writing it, in case I accidentally copy another writer's style. Otherwise I read pretty much what I write;

mainstream and SF in nearly equal proportions (and usually alternating between the two), though I read a bit of popular science, history and other non-fiction too. My hobby away from writing still means staring at a screen; music. I have a wonderful, stunningly powerful program called Logic 7 running on a different Mac in another room, linked up to a decent keyboard, a scattering of other sound and processing modules, a mixing desk and good pair of speakers. I hill walk to get out and away but then that's where I often get my best ideas, so it's still about writing.

Charles Baxter

As I have gotten older, I have started to read more history and political analysis. Watching the catastrophe of the current Bush Administration, I have been driven to read Tactitus' *Annals of Imperial Rome*. I read whatever I feel like reading at the time, whatever 'speaks to my condition', as the Quakers say.

Andy Brown

I try and do all sorts of things to *not think* full stop! My mind is just too busy sometimes: 'I have need to busy my heart with quietude', Rupert Brooke wrote, and I fully sympathise. I need some stillness in my life to do anything properly. When I want not to think, I'll go and do some exercise in the gym, or swim fifty lengths, or go and dig my allotment (which is enormously therapeutic), or go for a long rambling walk. More often than not I'll pick up one of my instruments and play some music, write a new tune, sing some songs. Or listen to some records and dance about a bit. Cookery is good too. I also like fishing: you just sit on the side of the water and stare at your float. It's very, very Zen.

When I want to think, I'll read. Anything and everything. At the moment I've set myself the task of reading all of Dickens' novels (I started it because my colleague is *always* talking about Dickens, but I'm a total addict now myself). I've nearly completed the job and am half way through *Bleak House* to round it all off. I read a lot of contemporary novels too, as well as re-reading favourite books from the past. And then there's all that non-fiction to read too, particularly books about the natural world. I've just been re-reading the sublime Annie Dillard, *Pilgrim at Tinker Creek*, a book that changed my life. Richard Mabey's *Nature Cure* has just been closed too; a superb exposition on depression and the redemptive power of the natural world.

As for poetry, I read it all the time – for pleasure, to review, for teaching, to clear my eyes and lift my spirit. I try and read some poems aloud every day – there are poetry books stationed all around the house, though my main library is in my office at work. I've just been re-reading Eliot (having listened to a recording of 'Prufrock...' laid-over a Portishead track on YouTube), and Pound's *Cathay* poems, because I adore them. But this morning I also read Mary Oliver's *House of Light* from cover to cover before I got out of bed, her beautiful evocations of the natural world, and I've just discovered Brigit Pegeen-Kelly's extraordinary poems collected in *Song* and *The Orchard*. I'm always on the search for new poets, to read and enjoy, and to use in teaching, and so probably read at least one book of poems a day. Is this the 'obsession' you were alluding to earlier?

Maggie Butt

Reading has always been a huge pleasure for me, and I can't imagine the word 'holiday' without the word 'books'. In term time there's never enough time to read, and I have a big pile of books on my bed-side table which get about half an hour a night before I go to sleep. I tend to alternate novels and poetry collections, and also subscribe to a lot of poetry magazines, which seem to all arrive at once and have to wait their turn. This reading is pleasure and brain-food.

Then there are the books I read as research for my writing, or in order to up-date my teaching book lists.

I wouldn't say that much of this reading is deliberately connected with my writing, but it certainly feeds, sustains and sometimes inspires it.

Jack Epps Jr.

I read to relax. Currently, I'm reading a lot of history. I've become fascinated with the Korean War because it's the forgotten war and not one wants to talk about it. So many heroes, so many dead, so forgotten. Since I was an English major, I get bored really fast if the prose isn't inspired. Michael Chabon is a terrific writer I greatly admire. His prose is outstanding.

I don't read anything about the Industry. I did that when I was starting out. I read two newspapers every day, *The Los Angeles Times* and *The New York Times*. I have to understand and feel the world zeitgeist so I can write and stay connected to the audience. I'm not trying to second guess world culture and attitudes, I just want to be connected to it.

I am very involved in the lives of my children and my family. We are close and do a lot together. Very fulfilling and also insightful. I don't write about my family, but I'm sure I absorb a lot of their emotions. Everything seeps into the work.

Nadine Gordimer

Never read work connected with what I happen to be writing. Read whatever I am drawn to. Don't have any conscious escape from work in progress, but the *train – train* of daily life, good and bad, serves the purpose.

Kate Grenville

I read mostly non-fiction these days – popular science, history, archaeology, ecology. As far as work goes, I've found it better on the whole not to do paid work too close to my 'real' work. When I've written stories etc for a specific market and brief I'm conscious of playing dangerously with spoiling something in my own imagination. I enjoy teaching writing and that's been my main source of income – but I find workshopping stories rather deadening – on the other hand short writing exercises are energising for everyone in the class.

Nessa O'Mahony

I read whatever I can lay my hands on. During the PhD, I felt extremely guilty about reading anything that wasn't directly related to my subject matter. Since then, I've been thrilled to be able to read anything at all. I never read enough poetry, I admit, and still tend to read more fiction, even though I principally write poetry.

Ruth Padel

I work very hard and tend to have to read things I can use in some way for the current work in hand. But I always need a novel on the go too.

Robert Pinsky

This provides a good counter-balance to my previous answer. The newspaper is important to me. To someone else it might be birding, books, or gardening, or Napoleonic history, or Marxism, or early anthropology. But on the record, great writers know their art along with worlds outside their art: for Homer, armed combat; for Chekhov, worldly conversation. I imagine that Wallace Stevens, who wrote so well about imagination and mortality, gained some insight or balance in those subjects by knowing how the forces of imagination and mortality manifested themselves in claims law and the manners of an insurance company. Just as William Carlos Williams clearly gained a lot from his studies and daily work as a physician.

I am biased toward the newspaper – not only for politics, material like the recently discovered lies and cynicism of the Bush administration, but also for the trivialities, pettiness, stupid preoccupations of one's time. I value the newspaper (my metonymy for various sources of contemporary information) but great writers have ignored it. Great writers do not ignore the great writing of the past.

At my point in life, re-reading is a great pleasure, and one feels entitled to it. All due respect to young poets – sometimes, rather than reading their new books, I choose to read around in Ulysses or the poems of Dickinson for an hour or so.

Philip Pullman

I read whatever I feel like reading, and only for as long as it interests me. I long ago stopped feeling guilty about not finishing books that were boring me. If you looked at my bookshelves you'd find evidence of omnivorousness, and few patterns; though there is a lot of poetry, and quite a lot of history, and a fair amount of writing about science. You'd also find a lot of thrillers. You'd also find a lot of books with a bookmark partway through. As for non-reading activity, I play the few musical instruments lying about the house very badly, and I make things out of wood fairly well.

Tom Shapcott

I have always been a voracious reader. I like to keep abreast in contemporary literature, do I try to keep current with what is being published in Australia (including all fields, except perhaps sport and female-detective fiction). I read fairly widely in contemporary American and English literature. I have some knowledge of recent Canadian and New Zealand literature, but not nearly as much South African. Modern European poetry (in translation) and Asian too. I try to maintain a mix, so histories, current affairs, and things like biographies or autobiographies are always of interest. If my own writing (mainly in prose, but not always) demands research, well I throw myself into it. I think it was WHITE STAG OF EXILE that taught me the joys of research.

William Tremblay

What do you read that feeds your ability to write?

Aside from daily newspapers, magazines, the books I read cover a wide range of topics. This summer [2008] I've read books on neurophysiology and consciousness, the *Popol Vul* and the Mayan glyphs, an anthology of contemporary Mexican poetry, and many books and articles on all aspects of screenwriting which have led me to reflect that while movies may depict they cannot describe, i.e. what people read for is the voice of a poet or story-teller whereas in film 'voiceover' can be a crutch, a distraction, a statement of the obvious but not very often a good thing.

In sight-reading a graphic novel like *Watchmen* I have seen degrees of specificity that language rarely achieves. Or, another way to appreciate the difference in art forms is to recall the story that F. Scott Fitzgerald was accosted in his office in Hollywood by a studio executive who stuck his head in the door and said, 'Mr. Fitzgerald, we cannot film adjectives!' Thinking about making everything palpably visual has led me to reflect that writing is comparatively abstract; I look back on this latest sentence, e.g., and I realize that I just string a series of words together and I convey an idea involving a contrast. How would I convey that in a movie? How could I use that answer in writing a poem?

What I'm suggesting here is that sometimes as a way of feeding your process it may be helpful to consider other art forms to get a handle on language and writing. Indeed, one leading idea from the late twentieth century is that when free verse arrived it had to borrow ideas of form from other fields – the telegraph message, [STOP], the structure of a baseball game, warfare, &c.

Xu Xi

I am a news junkie so I do tune in pretty 24–7. But on writing-reading, only once in my life did I take a job that involved creative writing (as a copywriter of commercials and ads) and that killed it for my fiction, as much as I liked working in an agency. After that, I refused to ever take a job that so interfered with writing. Teaching creative writing is a close second for killing my love of reading whatever comes across my radar, because I find myself reading a lot of things I might not have chosen to read just to stay informed for work (writing craft books, certain titles and authors that a lot of students are drawn to, genres or forms I might not have had any inherent interest in – the short short for instance, etc.)

I am a less keen reader than when I was a young writer and read pretty much everything. For one thing, I often don't bother finishing novels and ones that will hold my attention throughout are the ones that make it to my greatest hits list now (whereas I read everything to the end before in the interest of educating myself). But I still look for the reading that sparks something in me that says *yes,* this is why this whole business matters.

Yes I do consciously go to the gym (I have become a gym rat in recent years) because that is the most non-writing thing I can do. Everything else seems writing related somehow.

* * *

Reading for pleasure rates highly with the writers in *Inside Creative Writing.* 'I read to relax' says Jack Epps Jr. 'Reading has always been a huge pleasure for me,' says Maggie Butt, 'and I can't imagine the word "holiday" without the word "books"'. This is fortunate: it would have been awful to discover that in this (or any!) selection of writers most found reading to be a terrible labour!

The writers here often point to two things also: 1. reading something different to the genre they most often write and 2. reading widely, including an amount of non-fiction and at least some reading of the popular press. Jack Epps Jr. is 'reading a lot of history', and Charles Baxter notes history and 'political analysis' among his reading materials. Kate Grenville, who has indeed written fiction with an historical dimension, also says she reads works of popular science, archaeology and ecology. Nessa O'Mahony reads 'whatever I can lay my hands on', while Robert Pinsky notes that the newspaper is important to him, and not just for the political reporting. This is not to say that works of creative writing don't appear in the creative writers' reading, and Robert Pinsky's 'great writers do not ignore the great writing of the past' reminds us that some element of exposing ourselves to excellence in our field is common.

What would be productive would be our consideration of a time frame of creative writing and reading – (a) that material being read while a creative writer is commencing something, and (b) that being read while we are in the middle of writing a longer piece of work and (c) that being read towards the concluding stages. We'd also need to consider if playwrights read differently to fiction writers, screenwriters to poets.

References to the reading of the popular press strike me as relevant to recalling the broader sense of human reading. I wonder, in passing, if this is a version of our reading of faces, our reading of the weather, our reading of situations and moods in the natural world?

Could it be that we creative writers, being frequently voracious readers, are also voracious readers of context, intention, attitude? That is, could creative writers be engaged in a heightened version of our routine, primal human reading? Because we are engaged with reading in this heightened way, are creative writers also useful providers of reading techniques, experienced reader-guides to how humans can engage with that which is around them?

This might claim too much. But just as the painter or filmmaker, the actor, the musician or the ceramicist, picks up on the shapes or movements or the sounds or contours of our world so the creative writer picks up on the ways of reading it, the language contained in it, and from that builds the bridge between human reading and the written word.

Reflection

How does your reading compare to that mentioned by the writers? Do you have particular genres or forms of writing that you most often read?

Taking the wider sense of human reading as your context, can you describe any reading circumstances that seem to you to have been very significant in your life?

Exercise

The term 'literacy' is often used to refer to the ability to read and write. There's a whole cultural, national and international history to consider in relation to the ideal and idea of literacy. But I wonder if there might be a 'creative writing literacy'? That is, if you were asked to consider what it would be to be literate in the field of creative writing what might it entail (try outlining this in a short paragraph, as if you were communicating this to someone who is entirely unaware of this creative writing literacy – suggested word length for this exercise: 200 words)? Some of this relates to earlier discussions knowledge and skills, but it also relates to ideas about how we read and how written language performs as art and communication.

12
Other Practicalities

Because many people reading this book will no doubt be thinking about creative writing in terms of practicalities, are there any practical notes you'd be willing to add? For example, I'm always intrigued by the notion that all writers move from one finished work to the next finished work, thoughts about the next one neatly beginning after writing of the previous one is concluded – when it seems more common for writers to move in and out of works, over time, some writing going from start-to-finish in a linear fashion, some starting and then being interrupted by other things, other projects, more thoughts, life, before getting to the final stretch.

The practical considerations in creative writing are numerous, and the majority of creative writers work independently, and work singularly. So we each frequently deal with these practicalities on our own. We could say that some creative writers are 'contract workers', on the basis that they are contracted by someone to deliver a completed work. But a great many more write entirely on speculation, and more still solely because they enjoy writing. These writers often undertake their creative writing without any regular input from anyone – except themselves.

If many of us creative writers enjoy our independence, it is also the case that this frequently throws us back onto the practicalities of our undertaking. We move from one task to another, making decisions about what we feel is successful and what feel isn't, more or less privately engaged with questions of how to continue and how to complete the things that we're doing.

Is this unique? In the arts, not really because so many artists in the world are not doing what they do as contract or freelance workers (that is, as a profession), but are pursuing their personal interests, without any real need or obligation to benchmark their actions or understandings against an industrial, cultural, societal or, indeed, artistic norm. The same independence of action and mind is also found in sport (certain sports pursued on an amateur basis, at least), where the practicalities of how to do it, how you might enjoy doing it, and what obstacles might be faced in you undertaking it, are often located almost exclusively in yourself, and the decision about how much external influence is sought is located in your own temperament.

Let me speculate a little that the reason quite a few of those undertaking creative writing as a pastime not as a profession find their level of enjoyment decreases, or that they eventually cease to write creatively at all, is because day-to-day practicalities overwhelm their writing. Because those writers are not *required* contractually or financially to continue, and often have a relatively sparse support network for what they do, they simply lose the impetus.

All this would be so self-evident as to be worthy of no comment at all, except that it reflects just how little our engagement with the arts is supported by day-to-day modern life. Certainly educationalists, and even entire national governments, tout the importance of human creative life (much as they tout the importance of exercise in the pursuit of human well-being). But day-to-day considerations, including earning a living, place far more pressure on the casual creative writer *not* to write they do offer encouragement to continue to write.

So what light can we shine here in their chapter on the practicalities of creative writing? What practicalities might contribute productively to our creative writing, regardless of whether we are undertaking it professionally or casually?

Some of the problem arrives because creative writing is an undertaking that is so based in an individual, and in an individual disposition, that it comes with very few transferable guidelines and, as noted, a relatively low level of network support.

All manner of 'how to' books and writers' interviews books don't quite deal with our real-life practicalities. Even though both professional and casual creative writers sometimes draw on the inputs of writers' groups, editors, teachers, friends and family, ultimately each creative writer faces the contest that arrives when sitting down in front of a blank screen or page.

Practicalities come in many forms. Frequently, the pressing issue of time and the arrangement of time is one of them. 'Arrangement' meaning how we balance our interest in creative writing with the general pressures within society to not really devote much time to doing it! The professional creative writer can at least use their working day to counter that situation. They can speak to themselves (or others) on behalf of their career need to continue writing. But the casual creative writer – let's address something of what they can do.

Here's where issues of practicality become issues of simply ending up not writing at all. The casual creative writer can often benefit greatly from creating a roadmap of their creative writing in order not to lose it. That is, a written or drawn map of what you are doing, and how will you complete it.

In general, the idea that a creative writer heads down one mapped road with one writing task in mind is a massive oversimplification, often an outright untruth. Writers move about their territory, they travel in many directions at once. The pursuit of one work melds with the pursuit of another. A new idea emerges while working on a previous one. One work fails the exact moment before or after another one has wonderfully succeeded. I've mentioned elsewhere the restriction that the notion of a rigid chronological pattern to the actions of writers places on genuinely grasping creative writing. Creative writing does not work in that rigid way.

Not doubt at all that to be a creative writer you must be writing. But how you do it, when you do, and where you do it is part of your writerly independence, your choices.

There's a wonderful photo on the cover of Jane Grayson's book *Vladimir Nabobov*.[1] It shows Nabokov reclining in the front seat of a car, alone, his back against the car door, window open, writing on one of his index cards, clamped by his thumb over another of his index cards. Whether he is writing fiction or engaged in the recording of some evidence of a butterfly, renowned lepidopterist that he was, is not stated (though probably discoverable, if we sought out the original photo). But to an extent it doesn't matter. What the photo seems to be saying is: 'Vladimir Nabokov, grasping time, travelling somewhere, moving amongst his writing'.

Dealing with matters of place and time – aspects of our writerly habitats – are practicalities. Creating a sense of movement, a journey somewhere from starting a project to finishing it, is a practicality. Plotting out a personal roadmap for doing this, even if only in your head, is practical assistance for this. And recall, rarely ever will anyone consistently ask you to write! Even the most famous professional creative writer, contracted to write, expected to write and celebrated for their writing, is at so many points left to their own motivation, their own desire, their personal reasons for writing.

Practicalities, I've said, come in many forms, and comparative approaches to investigating these practicalities offer promise of revealing much. As yet, you'll find relatively few published comparative investigations. For example, comparative studies of how our personal writing roadmaps differ from one creative writer to another, or from one creative writing project to another. There are not really any of those studies, as yet. Studies where we can see a writer's decision-making, influenced by personal choice as well as cultural context, by the aspects of one project or another. No, not yet any of those either.

There is more work to be done in exploring creative writing, and much of that work is practically intriguing as well as pressing. To choose one example: information about the instruments we use for writing (individual books of writers' interviews might touch on this, but there's a lack of concerted comparative studies of creative writers' use of various writing technologies, from a pencil to a computer, a cell phone and more, and the impact of these on their ways of composing, perhaps their ways of thinking).

Indeed, there remains much to be explored and compared in the field of creative writing. Practicalities include not only our technological tools of writing but our compositional tools, our ways of undertaking, our methods of progressing. Casual writer or professional, there's every indication that creative writing doesn't occur without some form of human effort – what type and style of effort, or the techniques individual writers have developed for applying that effort, has not yet been widely examined. This chapter aims to explore some of this.

* * *

Iain Banks

Easy. Writing is like everything else; the more you do it, the better you get. It's all about the three 'P's: practice practice practice. My other piece of advice would be to get stuff finished; write to the end and then start polishing. Don't worry if that first paragraph isn't perfect and keep going over and over and over it before tackling the next para. Finish the story first. Then revise. And remember that there's no such thing as a perfect novel. A perfect poem is possible, if it's short; you can imagine there's no change, either additive or subtractive, that could improve it, however with all but the shortest of short stories, that's not even a possibility regarding a piece of prose. And do your homework; check out the Writers and Artists' Yearbook or whatever to make sure you know you're submitting material to the right place.

Charles Baxter

All my practicalities are on display in my two books concerning writing, BURNING DOWN THE HOUSE and THE ART OF SUBTEXT: BEYOND PLOT.

Andy Brown

Trust the world and, even though they are slippery things, use the words you mean and mean the words you use. Remember that writing, like living, is a process, and an overbearing attention on yourself, or on the products of your writing will destroy the creative energy that fuels those processes.

Maggie Butt

I suppose the most practical note is to say never be satisfied with your writing, seek out help wherever you can find it, keep reading, keep writing, and never give up.

I certainly don't write in a linear fashion, finishing one poem before embarking on the next. They over-lap in many draft forms before coming to a final rest. I can be writing one when a thought or a phrase for another pops into my head. It would be terrifying to finish a poem without any idea of others which might be in an embryonic stage.

Jack Epps Jr.

This is a huge question. This would take a book to respond to. When I finish a work I'm usually really sad. A bit melancholy. I feel a loss of a sort of friendship I have developed with my characters over a period of months. I have had an intimate relationship with this person/character and it is sometimes difficult to let them go. And we have been alone together. And now I have to share them with others who will not be so kind and understanding. Really the hardest part.

Everyone needs to find their process. I'm a linear writer. I believe in cause and effect plotting. What happens in one scene leads to the next scene, and so on and so on. Rewriting is difficult because there is a lot of emotional connection between my scenes. But I'm a good rewriter because I jump into the script and am willing to make big changes. The first draft is mine, the second draft is the studios. From then on I do what needs to be done to get the work mounted without destroying the heart. If I have to destroy the heart, then I'm not the right person to rewrite the screenplay.

My practical advice is ask a lot of questions before you begin writing. Even if you are going to start on page one and see where it goes, you need to have materials, characters, their inner stories, to work from. Read a lot of screenplays. Good one and bad ones. You learn more from the bad ones. The mistakes are clear and they make you feel better about your own writing.

Write to your strengths. If you're great with dialogue, then let it carry the story. Don't lay a heavy plot on something that relies on repartee and banter. If you write great plots, then don't stop the train for a clunky characters story. Find your strength and write to it. Work on your weaknesses, but highlight what you do best.

And lastly, write lean. Not too much description, no long speeches. Remember, you are reading to be read before it moves onto the next stage. A fast read is the best read. Tighten descriptions. Don't try to impress people with your writing skills, impress them with your storytelling skills.

Nadine Gordimer

Only answer is that for 11. [**143**].

Kate Grenville

My only rule of thumb is, if it feels as if I'm forcing it, move onto something else. So if I get to a point in a book when it's going dead and I'm just forcing it along, I'll turn to another project for a while, or go away & do some research around it. For me there's nothing neat in any aspect of writing – projects overlap, get put away & taken out, transform over time. I never start a book at the beginning, always just plunge in to a bit I'm looking forward to writing and build out from those high-energy bits. I usually have only the vaguest idea what a project will be when I start – *The Secret River* for example started as a small-scale bit of family history for the archives.

Nessa O'Mahony

I'm not sure if poets are quite so linear as that, unless they are deliberately working on a themed sequence or, of course, a verse narrative. Yet they sometimes find that unconsciously they have been working to a pattern, something they discover when assembling poems for a full collection.

Ruth Padel

At present I have so many projects backed up waiting, a perpetual log jam of guilt about things not yet finished, that I can't think about that. I have to focus furiously on one thing at a time.

Robert Pinsky

Everybody is different. I like to have three or four projects of different kinds going, so that I can rebel against some of them, disobey or betray some of them, in order to cut class (is 'playing hooky' only an

Amercanism?) and work on the one piece of writing I fool myself into considering forbidden.

Philip Pullman

Well, you're right, of course. Everything overlaps. A good thing too. Projects have furtive affairs with each other when my back's turned, and their children turn up a little later, with healthily mixed genes, making a noise and a mess and demanding pocket-money. But it's good to have children around the place, even with the noise and the mess. God, in whom I don't believe, save us from primness, exclusiveness, neatly delineated borders, and the fear of 'contamination'.

Tom Shapcott

With novels, I usually have two I am working on together. Poetry can come any time. I find it useful and even stimulating to move from one genre to another; but then I have had lots of practice! Each form has different and quite distinct demands.

William Tremblay

How do you work, intensively on one piece, or do you work on more than one piece at a time?

I am currently at work on a book of poems entitled *Director's Cut: Scenes from the Painter's Life* which is about David Alfaro Siqueiros. I'm also writing a screenplay entitled *Fire with Fire*, which is about David Alfaro Siqueiros. As I previously mentioned, I'm also at work on a screen adaptation of my novel, *The June Rise,* which is about Joseph Antoine Janis, a mountain man who married First Elk Woman, sister of Red Cloud, the Oglalla war chief. Meanwhile, I'm trying to find the money to make a docu-drama about the Mexican illegal immigrants who work in the Yakima valley of central Washington state entitled *Because I Don't Have Wings* (Por no alas tener) as well as working with several of my former students on various writing projects, helping them to edit books they hope to find publishers for. Sometimes what happens is that I am able to translate one idea from one project onto another. This is the way I work. I also understand that other people work in different ways. What is the right way to work for you? Only rolling your sleeves up and getting to work will answer that question. Learn by doing; it's an old idea. Look at the work, not your fears; that's also an old idea but not so often heard. Look at the trail up the mountain, not the chasm.

Xu Xi

It's not linear if I look at all the different writing I do. Above [previously] I described my novel writing process insofar as how I do move from one book to the next (with some overlap but not much). But in the mix of stories and essays, and, these days collaborations I write, I do go in and out of things, as the progress of any given piece is quite unpredictable. Deadlines also create false urgency because some editor has been promised a thing, and that will force me to work on something because of deadline creep.

* * *

Evidence here suggests that the non-linear, many faceted, multiple project nature of creative writing is common enough to be the creative writers' norm. The writer who works linearly, works with singular intention, works uninterrupted and relentless, is rare. Kate Grenville mentions that her 'only rule of thumb is, if it feels as if I'm forcing it, move onto something else', while with Tom Shapcott's novel writing he usually has 'two I am working on together'. Philip Pullman too mentions that his 'projects have furtive affairs with each other when my back's turned, and their children turn up a little later, with healthily mixed genes, making a noise and a mess and demanding pocket-money'. And Robert Pinsky says that he likes to 'have three or four projects of different kinds going, so that I can rebel against some of them, disobey or betray some of them'. Alternatively, Iain Banks says that 'my other piece of advice would be to get stuff finished; write to the end and then start polishing', though this is advice about completion not necessarily about whether you might be working on more than one thing at a time.

While it's satisfying creatively and critically to find that in asking a question like this the answers concur with your own

thoughts, it is perhaps healthy to be wary of coming to an immediate conclusion. Reflecting on this question suggests much harks
back to a consideration of creativity itself. The oft quoted psychologist, Mihaly Csikszentmihalyi, says in his chapter 'The Work
of Creativity' that:

> The creative process starts with a sense that there is a puzzle
> somewhere, or a task to be accomplished. Perhaps something is
> not right, somewhere there is a conflict, a tension, a need to be
> satisfied. The problematic issue can be triggered by a personal
> experience, by a lack of fit in the symbolic system, by the stim-
> ulation of colleagues, or by public needs. In any case, without
> such a felt tension that attracts the psychic energy of the per-
> son, there is no need for a new response. Therefore, without a
> stimulus of this sort, the creative process is unlikely to start.[2]

For Csikszentmihalyi, then, a puzzle or a task sets things in
motion. If that is the case most creative writers would be entwined
in multiple puzzles, simultaneously, undertaking multiple tasks.
The idea of this might lead us to wonder how anyone would actually survive doing this, day in and day out! Or, perhaps, that's
exactly the attraction – the puzzle solving, the variety of tasks we
undertake in creative writing.

Some of this discussion returns us to Chapter 5, and considering
the ways in which drafting is itself a systemic activity, informed
by a creative writer's sense of how one part of that activity relates
to another – writing, researching, editing, with no fixed division
between these things.

Having more than one project in motion, dealing with more
than one puzzle, undertaking more than one task, would seem
both possible and usefully complementary if the activities of
drafting occur at varying times. Writers thus move between one
moment of one project and one moment of another. But what also
seems very likely is that creative writers organise their place and
time, their habitat as discussed in Chapter 8, to respond to their
specific undertakings.

Csikszentmihalyi does note that 'every domain has its own
internal logic, its pattern of development, and those who work
within it must respond to this logic.'[3] While 'must' seems a little

draconian, there does seem a good case for saying that those who work within creative writing '*will* respond to this (its) logic'. Although this responding is subject to our individual personalities, it does mean making creative writing intrinsic to our lives – and this response in effect does represent a distinctive world view. That is, the world view of creative writers.

Reflection

How often do you write, and what practical issues arise? I'm not talking about drafting issues here – something we considered in Chapter 5. Rather, what life issues arise and how do you incorporate or negotiate them? If you were to imagine the ideal scenario for your creative writing, what would it be – remembering, of course, that relatively few creative writers now, or throughout history, have ever worked only on their creative writing, so we've long been at work on this?

Exercise

If creative writers most often have more than one project somewhere in their midst, how might this be beneficial? What might be the potential pitfalls? If you've experienced this multiple project scenario is it possible now to create a roadmap of how it worked or didn't work? (Suggested length for this exercise: 500 words.) Also, try mapping this out in graphic form: connections, intersections, directions of travel, results achieved (use a 'mind-map' approach for this). How does this look?

Reflection

Someone asks you to write a poem or a short story for a collection to be published relatively soon. You agree, but this request comes at a particularly busy time in your life. What do you do to get the writing done? Is 'writing to order' in this fashion possible for you? What is entailed in this kind of request – for you, as a writer?

13
Exploring Creative Writing Exercises

I don't want to leave this question until very last, in case the answer is 'No' or 'Not really', which is fine, of course. But, hopefully ... Were you to suggest a brief activity someone might undertake that has the potential to reveal something about creative writing, what might it be? Anything. I remember, for example, someone saying 'try some first draft writing without pausing to think too much about it, and see what happens', and though I ended up with a mess it did release some ideas. Someone else said, in talking about creating a voice in fiction, 'try writing as if you're acting a part'. Anything at all?

This chapter clearly makes the suggestion that creative writing can be taught, but some might say this suggestion involves a rather big assumption. The position adopted here is entirely up front. It'll be obvious to you that this entire book proceeds on that big assumption.

Whether creative writing can be taught is one of those debates re-visited often, despite the fact that there are now tens of thousands of creative writing courses being offered in a wide variety of educational settings, worldwide. What frequently occurs in these 'can be taught/can't be taught' debates is that commentators return to questions of what is actually meant by teaching and what is meant by creative writing. As that indicates, this couldn't go any more to the 'core' of discussions about the nature of creative writing. At that core interesting arguments emerge.

Beginning on one side of the debate – that creative writing *can* be taught – what many ask is what *should* be taught? After all, given that creative writing is such an eclectic activity, what constitutes a creative writing programme? What constitutes levels of learning and levels of achievement? Where should any one course begin, what should it entail and how should it progress? In fact, not only how should any creative writing programme progress but how should someone progress *through* a programme and what should be the end result of doing it?

That's one portion of a discussion, on one side of the debate. On the other side of the debate – that creative writing *can't* be taught – what most often focuses attention is just how anything like creative writing *could* ever be taught. The suggestion, roughly paraphrased, is that rather than teaching it the best that we can hope to achieve is a level of tyro writer encouragement, some exposure to successful works of creative writing and, to the extent that it can be achieved, some technical instruction that alerts emerging writers to the tools at hand, even if it is not possible to ensure they can fully use them.

It is unfair to present the case for the 'opposing/can't be taught' side, while openly declaring that creative writing can indeed be taught. However, there are a few elements of this 'opposing' argument already present in previous chapters, and their reasoning is not entirely unsound. These are some of those arguments:

1. That knowledge in creative writing is not just technical knowledge, not just knowledge of writing actions or the potential end results of actions, but is also combined with a way of thinking, and responding, and with the inherent emotional and imaginative make up of individuals, which is simply possessed and can't be learnt;
2. That the imagination is not something that is easily reduced to a set of schemes of study but that needs an openness of time and place and result that teaching situations can't provide;
3. That part of the reason for undertaking creative writing in the first place is the condition of self-learning that a formally taught creative writing class can't easily support, especially if there is a need to set formal tasks and assess a student's ability

to undertake these at a given time in a school or academic
year;

4. That the ideal of an individuality that impacts on behaviours
   of making represents the ideal of a singular, innate talent; and,
   significantly, talent can't be taught.

These few examples of arguments challenging the idea that creative writing can be taught are compelling. But the reasons why
this book – and the investigation in this chapter – proceed on
the basis that creative writing can be taught seem to me to be
stronger.

Responses to the arguments, above, run along these lines:

1. Knowledge in creative writing is, most definitely, more than
   technical knowledge. Truly, too, its responsiveness relates to
   questions of the mind, imagination, personality, to instinct
   as well as to intellect, to mood, reasoning and consciousness.
   Other areas of human endeavour also draw on these things,
   and when we explore, and teach, creative writing we seek to
   connect the surface of creative action, in this case, with the
   under-surface of thinking, understanding and responsiveness.
   That knowledge is often more than technical knowledge is uni-
   versal, not specific to creative writing.

2. Contemporary mass education does place pressure on time.
   This has actually been the case since education at a family,
   local or community level was gradually replaced by education
   at more centralised, institutional level. A good creative writing
   course, and an effective creative writing programme, will make
   room for the imagination, encourage imaginative exploration.
   Naturally, education and the imagination are, quite obviously,
   are not fundamentally in opposition.

3. Again, this is not a challenge to creative writing being taught,
   only a pointer to the fact that *how* it is taught must be actively
   addressed.

4. Finally, it is absolutely true that, as it has often been stated,
   'you cannot teach talent'. But this is not a claim in any form
   of education. Nor should it be that a creative writing education
   is expected to teach fame – by which I mean, how we define

success in creative writing should be carefully evaluated before rejecting the idea of teaching creative writing. It could be that what is being suggested is that you cannot make someone talented or famous, not that you cannot teach them to write creatively. The two things are not the same.

There are a great many deliberations on these issues in a great many places. To mention just one historical example, back in 1990 the well known literary journal *Mississippi Review* ran a Special Issue on teaching writing. Some of the indicative comments include these from James Gunn: 'What workshops teach is criticism. The most difficult part of learning to write is knowing when you have written well and when you have written badly.'[1] These, from Matthew Brennan: 'I'm not sure students can be taught to write literature, but they can be taught to read it.'[2]. And these from Kendra Kopelke: 'Once students become curious about what their own imaginations can teach them, writing becomes a way to get there.'[3]

The examination in this chapter is a teaching and learning examination, but it is somewhat more specific than whether creative writing can be taught. Simply, do any of the creative writers in *Inside Creative Writing* feel there is anything that immediately comes to mind that they can offer up to reveal something to someone about creative writing?

*   *   *

Iain Banks

I think I've kind of covered that above! **[153]**

Charles Baxter

Charles Dickens practiced in front of a mirror to get a sense of how his characters moved or behaved. I take walks. I take walks and try to see my characters. Yesterday, on a walk, I discovered that one of my characters wears dark glasses all day and in the evening, not because she wants to be cool, but because her eyes suffer from oversensitivity to light.

Andy Brown

Write openly. Don't censor yourself. Write like you're unafraid.

Maggie Butt

I sometimes find that a shift in perspective gives writing a good shake-up. So if you want to write about people trafficking (for example) and the third person just isn't working, try writing the letter home which the trafficked person would write if they could, try writing a phone call from the trafficker to the purchaser, try writing the thoughts of the car used for the people moving, or the dog who guards the victims. You might in the end return to the first version, but with new insight.

Jack Epps Jr.

One of the most important parts of creative writing in my opinion is to take yourself out of the process – take thought and consciousness out of the writing. There are any number of ways a writer can loosen up. I like to have characters tell me about their dreams. Write a stream of consciousness about what they would do, or where they would be, and what their life would be like in a perfect world. I let them tell me about themselves. I try to get into their voice and write from their perspective on the world. It's not the product, it's the process. Let it flow without worry about result.

I'm always looking for secrets and lies. What is hidden under the surface? What are they avoiding? Where is the pain located and how are they hiding it?

I don't like to start writing and see where I get or what comes out. Some people find this useful, but I find it a waste of time. That's my method. I'd rather free associate about a character or a situation, and see what comes out of it without worrying about context. Structure is very context oriented and needs to be done very specifically – consciously – but only after you know what the story is about and who is the main character. Structure by itself is an empty house. Once you know who lives in the house, you can design it around them.

I also answer pages and pages of questions about my story, world, character, relationship, and background. I spend a lot of time just thinking aloud on paper. Again, I do not self correct, but start to build aspects of the story and character that repeat or continue to grow. Let the themes emerge.

Start with the germ – inspiration and then grow it from there. A body on the beach. Why? Who is it? What happened the night before? What point is this in their life? What did they do for a living? Were they in love? Just ended? Who found them and what is their story? It's endless. Question after question until you know the answers.

Nadine Gordimer

Novels, stories: you are hearing your own voice, and must judge whether or not what is heard must somehow, some way, a right way for it, be told.

Kate Grenville

I'm a great believer in free writing – take an object or word and just start free associating onto the page about it – set an alarm for 3 or 5 minutes and just don't stop writing till it rings. At the start it will be neat and still controlled consciously but as time goes on you'll have to write 'this is silly, why am I doing this, I don't know what to write next...' and on the other side of that block will be a breakthrough – another subject – and that will be the subject you really want to think about – the thing that really matters to you.

It only works, though, if you really don't pause to think.

Nessa O'Mahony

A version of bibliomancy can be a good prompt for creative writing. Grab the nearest book, open it up at a random page, stab your finger on a random line, transcribe it and use it as the opening for a poem.

Ruth Padel

Sorry no idea.

Robert Pinsky

I've already said it: type up, with your own hands, an anthology: a definition by example, with many examples, of what you mean by words like 'poem' or 'poetry' or 'great writing'. Write it out! Performing that menial task may please the Poetry Gods and they may smile on you. And if nothing else, you have read something slowly, and you have asked yourself an important question.

Keep adding to it, and use it as a mirror: what does this book of yours lack? Is it all in translation? Nothing in translation? All contemporary and modern? What might you add to your range of instruments, by learning to love something new?

If you are feeling blocked, or bored with your writing – take a break by adding to your anthology. Your body will be in the writing posture, at the writing tools, and sometimes one thing leads to another.

And yes, of your examples, rapid, headlong composition can be useful.

Philip Pullman

I'm a bit impatient with this sort of thing. On a discussion forum I belong to an enquirer recently said that she would rather like to be a children's writer, but didn't know where to learn about it. Was there an academic programme she could join? Was it necessary to complete a course on writing for adults first before doing one on writing for children? I wanted to join in and say 'For God's sake, woman, just bloody well say *Once upon a time* and take it from there.' I didn't, because that would have been hurtful. No point in hurting anyone. No, I've got no useful tips. If someone wants to do it, they'll do it. If not, not.

Tom Shapcott

Be prepared, as I said, to let the computer of your sub-conscious play its part; try not to be too prescriptive to yourself when undertaking a major work. Setting – try to get accurate detail, this might involve research, which may actually give you fresh ideas or insights. Character: the cadence, of speech or even thought, is most important. Listen.

William Tremblay

Is there an exercise like automatic writing or borrowing acting techniques that helps a writer to improve?

Just knowing that there is an 'inside' which can and must be entered will lead toward inventing ways in. I'm sure there must be a book entitled *Writing from the Inside Out*. Isn't that connected to what Gerard Manley Hopkins was talking about when he invented the term 'inscape'?

In contrast, I'm also reminded of something Bly said years ago, something to the effect that the reason why American poets are obsessed with form and technique is that they are trying to invent a poetry-making machine so that even people with no imagination can write it. Robert has always had a way of being blatantly tough on the 'creative writing academy', but I think he's right in that there's no substitute for staying in the Rilkean void until the silence yields a word that grows into a poem.

Xu Xi

Walk (or act out) the action scene. The bad action I've read in student manuscripts often comes down to a lack of physical reality about what the people are supposed to be doing or an action that defies reality (A is looking into B's eyes when in the scene B's back is to A, etc.). In conjunction with this are the overly long sections of dialogue that impart information rather than reveal anything about the relationship between the characters, the conflict, or the characters themselves – I usually point to the curtain in Hemingway's 'Hills Like White Elephants' as the bit of action that keeps the dialogue on track and helps to move the story forward (that old chestnut is such a useful teaching story I find).

Those who have been involved in the teaching of creative writing at any point can probably reflect here on instances of success and failure in endeavouring to explain something about creative writing to someone else.

*   *   *

We might wonder if teaching writing technique is *always* going to be the most straightforward aspect of exchanging something between one writer and another – say, between one who is more experienced and one who is less experienced. Of course, as many will comment on both sides of the 'can be taught/can't be taught' debate, creative writing is much more than technique. So it is in all the arts. Kevin Volans, writing about the composition of music in an article entitled 'Dancing in the Dark: Craft and Composition', comments:

> Musical content can be understood, but it cannot be described in terms of an 'obsolete reality' (i.e. in terms of craft). Only through metaphor or images can we approach the topic.[4]

A literal 'description' as Volans calls it can't get close to the *content* aspect of music. For him it comes down to employing metaphor, a *shift in plane of reference*, rather than to a literal description.

Given the opportunity and assuming that we would like to offer something useful to another writer, then what 'something' would it be? The choice of plane of reference is important too, because if creative writing is operating on more than one plane then what would we prioritise? What would we find easy to transfer to others? How would we do this? For example, because creative writing is often operating on both an emotive and an informational plane – which of these would we prioritise? Can we explain both at the same time, what might be considering something from the plane relating to our *intellect* and something from the plane relating to our *feelings*?

This is a creative writing course query as well as a personal query. Many of those teaching of creative writing must surely have versions of this question on their minds regularly. Opinions will vary. Some might argue for technical information being the most important thing to offer up, because there needs to be some sort of identifiable ground-base on which to build and technical competence is relatively easily recognisable. But others might say that technical competence is far easier to develop than a writerly way of exploring the world, an engagement with our imaginations, and our ability to respond creatively to our thoughts, feelings and observations.

Some of the writers here have responded with regard to the technical aspects of creative writing, others have responded with regard to the elements of responsiveness to thoughts, feelings, observations. The role of the self, in either case, is prominent in these answers. Xu Xi offers something that might be said to combine technique and feeling: 'walk (or act out) the action scene,' she says. 'The bad action I've read in student manuscripts often comes down to a lack of physical reality about what the people are supposed to be doing or an action that defies reality.' Kate Grenville says she is 'a great believer in free writing', which is a form of connecting with the unconscious, a form of release from over thinking, it might be said. Jack Epps Jr. gives a specific example where he lets 'characters tell me about their dreams' and Tom Shapcott ends his comments by simply suggesting 'listen'.

Perhaps a good way to continue to speculate is to end with another quote from Kevin Volans, who says in his article:

> If you dance in the dark, you know exactly what you are doing. Where you are and where you are going is less clear.[5]

Reflection

Can you rank in any way the kinds of activities that seem to produce the best results for you in creative writing? By which I mean, if I was told I could pass on only one exercise to someone interested in creative writing, after some deliberation, I'd choose to pass on something to do with creating voice in fiction – because I personally find voice very interesting to explore, and I find works with distinctive voices enjoyable to read. If I was then given a second choice, I'd opt for something connected with the activity of free writing because, even though I might not use that exercise regularly in my own writing, I've been in a class where a creative writing teacher has pushed me to try the exercise and it worked for me, and for many others in that class.

The 'great debate' continues, and assuming readers of this book largely fall on the side of 'yes, it can be taught', ask a fellow writer if they are willing to share some aspect of creative writing with you, if you share some aspect with them. Assuming they are willing, see if in this mutual exchange you express yourselves in similar ways – what expressions do you both use, what aspects of creative writing do you gravitate towards?

Exercise

A bizarre division, but let's try it: thought or action? Create two columns, look at what activities the writers here have mentioned (if they have mentioned any) in their answers Which of these answers seems to be *thought* in creative writing, which seems to be about *action*? (suggested word length for this exercise: 500 words) Is the *thought/action* division possible or useful?

14
Asking Another Writer a Question

Were you to get the opportunity to ask another creative writer a question – any question at all – about what they do, what might it be?

First, a quick explanation, because this is the chapter where the writers generally give their shortest answers. That is partly the nature of my quizzing. It is not exactly out in left field to have asked these creative writers this, but it is hardly surprising that not every one of them had a question immediately on hand, or wished to ask one.

To put this in perspective, you can read this chapter as if it is that well-known manoeuvre towards the end of a job interview when the interviewers ask the interviewee 'Now we've asked you all those questions, is there anything you'd like to ask us?' Personally, I find I either want to reply: 'Sure, I'd like to go over all your questions again and get your own thoughts and explore some of the connections between each of you, and let's get to know each other a bit more.' Or, I want to answer: 'No thanks, I don't want to ask a thing. After all, we've set up a good system here, let's not ruin the moment.'

That said, I didn't actually ask the writers if they wanted to question me about anything I asked if they would want to question *any other creative writer* about any other thing. So, in a sense, I made it even more difficult because the first thing we might ask ourselves in that situation is 'which other writer and why?' That comes back to whether we creative writers are a well-defined group or a loose collection of individuals, whether we share a sense of communal identity. Does 'creative writer' represent an occupational category, a statement of a type of human undertaking, or a profession? Or is it all these things?

The concept of something being a profession is a powerful organiser of our human interactions (and, that is, the questions we might ask each other); when someone identifies themselves as an historian, a physician, a truck-driver, a computer programmer and so forth, whether they actually engage in these things as full-time jobs or only partake casually, the categories suggest a way in which we might interact and, in effect, the topics we might immediately explore.

Returning to music as a parallel art practice to creative writing, Jon Frederickson and James F. Rooney, writing in an article entitled 'How the Music Occupation Failed to Become a Profession',[1] summarise the traits commonly agreed as constituting a profession:

1. Possession of a specialized body of knowledge and techniques.
2. Establishment of a standardized course of training for imparting the specialized knowledge.
3. Testing applicants for knowledge and competence upon completion of training, followed by the granting of licenses to practice.
4. Licensed practitioners therefore hold a legal occupational status which guarantees them a monopoly over their sector of the market.
5. Autonomy from direct supervision and the substitution of collegial control in place of hierarchical control.

Creative writing would be seen by a reasonable number of people to display the first of these traits, but there'd be very few who'd recognise creative writing in the rest of these traits.

If creative writing is thus not a profession, at least according to these characteristics, then it must occasionally at least be an occupation. We can return to Frederickson and Rooney and hear something of an echo of creative writing here too:

> The music occupation created a market but failed to assert a monopoly over it. As a result, it became a semi-profession

which retained elements of both service occupations and professions: informal codes of conduct, education but no formal
credentials, structures to acquire status, and professional and
service occupation definitions of music as a commodity (aesthetic and utilitarian functions).[2]

Similarly, despite the growth of creative writing courses in universities and colleges, particularly throughout the later half of the twentieth century, there are absolutely no formal credentials required
in order to be considered a creative writer. As an art form it is not
'professionalised' in the same way as, say, architecture; and, as a
job, it is not subject to codes of conduct in the same way as, say,
many of the sciences and social sciences. To use Frederickson and
Rooney's terms, it can be essentially aesthetic, undertaken because
of a personal and occasionally occupational interest in the writing
arts, or it can indeed be applied to the utilitarian functions and
needs of other professions, other industries, first and foremost.

Some creative writers might live on the promise of acceptance of their next finished work by a publisher, a film company,
a theatrical company, others might only write casually with no
expectation or need for that kind of acceptance, but they write
nevertheless; still others might be employed to add flair to a greeting card, to be part of industries where 'writer' is one participant,
one role, in something much larger.

In these senses, 'creative writer' is more like many congrega-
tions than one congregation, more like many groups than one
autonomous, uniform group. Additionally, and it's already been
noted, not all creative writers – in fact, few creative writers – are
only involved in creative writing. Some work relatively close to
the occupational territory, themselves involved in publishing or
the media, for example, or in teaching budding writers in a university or college, or in some form of arts development. Still others work at a very great distance from creative writing, for much
of their daily lives entirely unconnected with it.

So what would you ask another creative writer? Well, that depends
on what kind of creative writer you are, and what kind of creative
writer they are. It is very much a person-to-person/one-to-one exercise. Similarly, what you might ask them might relate to an event
(for example, the publication of their new poetry collection, the

exercise they just suggested doing in a creative writing class, their recent creative writing award) or it might relate to the regular cycle of activities (for example, the day-to-day making of their work, their pattern of starting and finishing, some of the things this book has discussed concerning drafting, or how they move between critical awareness and creative practice) or it might relate to a long duration of writing history and context, something to ask that grounds their work in the history or context of a genre, a culture, a nation.

It is fascinating to sample what has been asked of creative writers by creative writers. Take some these from the well-known interview series in *The Paris Review*, where the series titles 'The Art of Fiction', 'The Art of Poetry', 'The Art of Theater' set the agenda but don't limit the scope. This – the poet Ted Berrigan interviewing Jack Kerouac:

> What encouraged you to use the 'spontaneous' style of *On the Road*?
> ... You have said that haiku is not written spontaneously but is reworked and revised. Is this true of all your poetry? Why must the method for writing poetry differ from that of prose?[3]

Or this, the poet Irish Dennis O'Driscoll interviewing the Australian poet Les Murray:

> Do you agree with Czeslaw Milosz that poems should be written 'under unbearable duress and only with the hope that good spirits, not evil ones, choose us for their instrument'?
> ... What aspects of your life were most crucial to your development as a poet?[4]

Or this, Robert Penn Warren being interviewed by Eugene Walter and Ralph Ellison:

> First, if you're agreeable, Mr. Warren, a few biographical details just to get you 'placed.' I believe you were a Rhodes Scholar –
> ... Did you start writing in college?[5]

The biographical, the technical, the philosophic or aesthetic, the cultural: if we were to wonder what it is that defines creative writers as a recognisable tribe we could probably come to the conclusion that it is, in fact, the lack of being one!

What we connect to, as writers, begins at the individuality of lives and of our writing practice. This moves somewhere between our natural curiosity of the kind found by one species in other members of that species and a desire not to intrude (or, indeed, a disinterest in doing so) into another life and possibly another set of practices that might be strikingly different to our own. This is the case even if the end results – whether poems, screenplays, novels, plays or any other form – have the physical appearance of having arrived from similar circumstances, related behaviours.

Sometimes we want to know a great deal, sometimes a little, sometimes nothing at all, and as we creative writers are neither a structured group, nor members of a professional guild, nor a political, cultural or economic mass, how we might respond to this is entirely personal.

* * *

Iain Banks

Hmm. I'm even less interested in my fellow writers than I thought...

Charles Baxter

The books are always the sufficient answer.

Andy Brown

Musicians think in sounds; sculptors think in volumes, shape, light and shadow; painters think in paint; cooks think in flavours; photographers think in light and shadow; potters think in clay. I get to talk to writers all the time, so I'd rather ask my question of these painters, filmmakers, sculptors, potters, and other types. *What do you think in, how, and why?*

Maggie Butt

Too many writers, too many questions.
   'So who was she, Will?'

'Can I have Mr Darcy's phone number?'

'Isn't it time you got a life Miss Dickinson? How about coming to the pub?'

(To almost anyone) 'What happens next?'

I wouldn't so much want to ask, as to sit at their side, to watch (entirely interfering with and spoiling the creative process) to see people at work on my favourite poems, what came first, what was their process, step by step, how, why...

But maybe that would be like the magician explaining the illusion, and maybe it would be spoiled.

Jack Epps Jr.

How do you get to the heart of your idea? What path do you take to find it? What is it that you hold in your mind while writing that helps you stay focused and consistent on this idea?

I'm also interested in process. Everyone has their own unique process – so there is no one way. I am also interested in how writers develop character. Again, everyone steps into character in their own way.

Nadine Gordimer

- - - -

Kate Grenville

When I meet writers, I find pretty soon the conversation comes around to that most important subject: how do you make a living while also writing?

Nessa O'Mahony

How do you maintain self-belief?

Ruth Padel

What do they read? And what books do they like of what they read? That says it all.

Robert Pinsky

I have that opportunity all the time. And I would make my question specific, not general. I would ask about a particular book, a certain poem, a specific line or passage. 'Robert, tell me why you begin a book of poems about the United States with a sentence about studious political prisoners in Africa?'

'Nikolai, what does the extended, mock-Homeric metaphor about the gentlemen in evening clothes resembling flies have to do with dead souls?'

Philip Pullman

I wouldn't. (See **84**)

Tom Shapcott

Probably I'd ask how many drafts, or how much of the intermediate ideas/thoughts had been eventually discarded.

William Tremblay

What one question would you ask another writer about how they do what they do?

I don't have to ask. It's there on the page. If not, then...

Xu Xi

Of Milton I would ask – If you really thought the devil was the bad guy, why the hell did you make him so memorable and God so blah?

* * *

A reader of a short story, the audience for a film, do they often ponder such a thing was created, who created it and in what circumstances? Do they think about the technical aspects of the making or about the personal origins of the story or the screenplay? Do they often start with a consideration of the writer and move towards the work, answering questions they might have by seeking out the work or works, because frequently they cannot easily seek out the writer? Does this depend on the kind of work that this is – does the reader of a limerick or indeed the purchaser of a greeting card wonder about the cultural context of its writer? Do the watchers of soap opera wonder about these things; or the readers of detective fiction? Are their larger debates that readers, who are not themselves creative writers, do not know or care much about?

> Our work is not necessarily so difficult or arcane, but it is highly specialized, and the questions we ask often make sense as part of larger debates that the uninitiated do not know or care much about.[6]

This quote is not about creative writing. It is about the writing of History. In his article entitled 'The Historian's Dilemma', Elliot J. Gorn discusses what he calls the need 'to stay immersed in the world yet maintain critical distance from it; how to engage our audiences with broadly important subjects yet not pander to them'[7].

It was the expressions 'not necessarily so difficult or arcane', 'high specialized' and 'the uninitiated do not know' that interested me, and made we wonder if Gorn's article on the writing of History might have any relationship to what the creative writers in *Inside Creative Writing* would answer to this, Question 14.

'Probably I'd ask how many drafts,' says Tom Shapcott. A pragmatic answer, but also an examination that is introspectively comparative. How many does it take someone to complete a story, a poem, on average? It's highly personalised. Alternatively Robert Pinsky would ask 'about a particular book, a certain poem, a specific line or passage.' A question about a finished work. And Ruth Padel would ask another writer what they read. For both Charles Baxter and William Tremblay answers to any questions they might like to ask should be found in the works themselves, while for Kate Grenville her question would reflect something of the nature of a creative writing life: 'how do you make a living while also writing?'

In 'The Historian's Dilemma' Elliott Gorn examines relationship between the 'marketplace' for books about history, the competitive academic marketplace as well as the popular literary marketplace, and how both impact on the 'profession'. You'll see where I am going with this. Whereas Gorn can turn to notions of structured professional practice, structured professional relation-ships, we might best turn to the relationships between the creat-ing and the audiences for what we create.

It is there that we come across this territory concerned with what Gorn calls 'debates' and 'caring' and it is there that lies the ideal of creative writing as something that brings together people from diverse backgrounds, with disparate interests and individual motivations.

It is exactly his approach to this that has the poet Paul Muldoon saying these things in his book, *The End of the Poem*:

> My theory is that, as it comes into being, the poem is marking and measuring itself against a combination of what it might now be and what it might yet become.[8]

Muldoon the poet knows that the 'coming into being' involves the creating activities of a poet, and no matter how much the non-poet reader is inserted, *post-event*, into the realm of reader-ship, into the receiving of a poem, and engaging with a poem, even to some measure re-writing the poem in their reading of it, the poet's recognition of 'coming into being' is that it came about because a poet *did something*.

That, in Gorn's sense, is the 'initiation', the 'specialised' activ-ity. And that is the essence of Muldoon's wondering too, and the reason he can strikingly summarise his feelings thus:

> It seems to me that all reading is, to a great or lesser extent, involved with speculation on what's going on, consciously or unconsciously, in the writer's mind, just as all writing is involved with speculation on what's going on, consciously or unconsciously, in the reader's mind.[9]

Exercise

The moment of truth, of course: what would you ask another crea-tive writer? Why? Try writing out that question (or questions), and venture an initial answer on the page (suggested length: 200–300 words). In other words, put yourself in the mind of another crea-tive writer and attempt to answer a question posed to them.

Reflection

Taking the comparative approach offered in this book, are there other examples of writers' interviews, non-comparative examples, where you have found questions you'd like to ask more than one writer? For example, in George Plimpton's interview of Ernest Hemingway, also for *The Paris Review*, Plimpton asked: 'Can you dismiss from your mind whatever project you're on when you're away from the typewriter?'[10] .I'd like to update that question for the twenty-first century, and ask a range of creative writers – not least because of a personal interest in whether composing on a computer, as many contemporary writers do, has changed relationships with material and thoughts surrounding that material.

Consider this, as a creative writer do you feel you can separate your 'writer' and 'reader' activities? That is, if you regularly read newspapers but as a creative writer are mostly a poet, do you feel you read newspapers as a poet or does your 'newspaper reader' identity have other aspects to that of your 'writer of poetry' identity? Has might this work, do you think?

15
Past, Present and Future

Finally, despite talk at various points, certainly from the last decades of the twentieth century onwards, that new communication technologies would zap the writing arts, more people seem to be writing creatively than ever before. I suppose I should have made that first sentence a quotation, and should now use the words 'Can you comment?' Simply, I wonder: are you generally positive about the future of the writing arts? Do you feel optimistic about creative writing, as an activity, and about the works that it produces?

You take a camera, perhaps that camera is also a mobile phone, you record some moving images, a film, you collect with this device or some other digital device, some sounds, you arrange these sounds in some fashion and edit them with these images, you load up these images and sounds somewhere, perhaps the Internet, or you send them from one phone to another. No need to wonder where the writing arts are in all this: they are largely absent.

It could easily be argued that creative writing was going to meet its stiffest competition when, in December 1895, Auguste and Louis Lumière entered *Le Salon Indien du Grand Café* in the *Place de l'Opéra* in Paris and held their first public screening of motion pictures. Moving picture devices had been invented prior to this, able to put pictures into a connective sequence, but this first public screening for which an admission fee was charged made something of a declaration of the future that those of the burgeoning twentieth century were soon to enthusiastically follow.

Many would argue that moving pictures – film and later television – were the most pervasive art form of the twentieth century and, leisure time being always limited, frequently displaced other art forms in the public's affections. The sheer intensity of some of the experiences brought about by the invention of moving pictures amazes even today – to imagine, that is, the capturing, creation and recreation of experiences as varied, as imaginative, as appealing to so many of our senses, as those that have come about because of the invention of moving pictures still can feel like stepping into the realm of science fiction rather than living in the day-to-day.

Creative writing has not been lost in this, and the history and evolution of creative media writing can be told with some enthusiasm by those who would argue for the importance of the writing arts in the world. But it is the predominance of the moving visual arts, as well as the music that has increasingly been connected with this, that is most obvious – not only the sometimes awe-inspiring sequences of images, invented or captured scene following scene, but also the movements between high art and popular, the creative cross-fertilizations and, indeed, the mass media cross-marketing of the end results, that is so incredible. If there is an ancient human enthusiasm for the written word then there is no argument at all about the modern human enthusiasm for the moving pictures.

Speculating on the future of creative writing doesn't stop there. In the mid-1970s, when personal computers were popularly demonstrated, and proprietary names such as Commodore, Apple and IBM began to become household names, few could have accurately predicted the variety and extent of changes in human lifestyles that these early devices can now be seen to have initiated. Like the motion picture camera and movie projector, the personal computer was more than a device: it brought along with it new ways of behaving as well as new methods of accomplishing tasks or of being entertained, and it brought these right into our domestic spaces. It is exactly at that intersection of utilitarianism and entertainment that the personal computer flourished converging, as it was increasingly known, previously detached activities. Shortly after the personal computer's arrival the typewriter, if not immediately the television, entered the graveyard of technological history.

These things might well pale when we begin to think of the technological revolutions – and the connected creative revolutions – initiated in the 1990s. Like the movie projector/camera and the computer, the Internet had existed for some years before it entered our personal space. It arrived in most of the Western world in the mid-1990s and, as it has spread, its impact on us all has been phenomenal.

The immeasurable amount of information and interactivity comes immediately to mind, but so do the challenges faced by the writing arts with the extent of new, alternative activities. Whether it is the immediacy of our access to varieties of the purely visual and aural – a domesticated extension of the challenges faced in the public realm after the birth of film – or whether it is the sheer volume of informational and entertainment traffic that the Internet/World Wide Web has brought about, the results for creative writing continue to be enthralling.

Now add to this the arrival and impact of mobile telephony, and the evolution of new languages and new concepts of writing connected with such mobile telephony ('txting' being the most obvious, and most pervasive language) and we might well wonder where the writing arts sit in *all* our human futures. This is even more pressing for creative writing than other forms of writing, precisely because of how these technologies influence and associate with our creative actions and thoughts, not solely because of their computative, electronic or industrial shapes.

Beyond doubt, though, the future is far from being only about the impact of new technologies. We can very briefly consider, with just a few examples, how many things have had an influence on the pasts and futures of the writing arts. Include here several dimensions of our changing human relationship with religion – the word 'creative' did once have almost entirely religious overtones. Also, the centuries of global expedition of reconnaissance and discovery whose enormous wider influence also, more specifically, changed many creative writers' sense of the world. Such journeying brought incredible new revelations long before the Internet counted out discoveries in vast numbers of digital pages. Changes in work–life patterns: these too have influenced who writes, when they write, what they write. Revolutions in the industry of bookselling, and changes in cultural taste brought about everything from migratory movements to cultural shifts instigated by revolutionary moments in the arts, the sciences, politics. Anyone reading this could list so many, many more things.

Therefore, looking at the impact of current technological developments as a singular if significant case study of changes that have affected creative writing, two things immediately appear obvious.

Firstly, that the writing arts are located in a catalogue of other choices, both in consuming and in creating terms, a catalogue of choices the size of which we have never experienced before. Secondly, that with all these choices, all of these other potential experiences, creative objects, human undertakings, more people are choosing to be engaged with creative writing than ever before. More people are able to distribute and discuss the results of their writing than ever before. And more people are able to do the creating and exchanging of their creative writing from their personal space, at their leisure.

* * *

Iain Banks

Well, painting is still around despite photography, and plays still get staged despite cinema, so I don't really understand what all the fuss is about. There will always be writing. It may manifest itself in different ways – film and TV scripts, computer games, whatever – but it'll be there as long as we are. I strongly suspect the novel will survive indefinitely, even if it doesn't represent the cutting edge of narrative technique.

Charles Baxter

I'd be more optimistic if the number of readers were going up, if book sales were going up, if there were a constant 'buzz' as we say in the States, about books. When the number of writers (but not of readers) goes up, you are simply in the presence of widespread cultural narcissism. Book sales are declining as the number of writers increases in quantity. That's not a good sign. Hey, everyone can be Tolstoy, right? No. Only Tolstoy could be Tolstoy. I'd be more optimistic if every one of my students had read WAR AND PEACE at least twice. Then I'd be happy.

Andy Brown

Yes, of course. I continue to read new books by new writers that excite me just as much as the canonical classics – that's very positive; very optimistic. Yes, you have to be selective – there are a lot of bad books too – but the field is lively and thriving and I don't see any reason why that will change.

I also have a job helping people to express themselves in words; how to be better readers; how to write. It would be a cynical teacher who didn't feel optimistic about that as an activity. I work very closely with people all the time, from all walks of life, who learn to be better writers, better readers, and who discover something deep about themselves and their relationships to the world through the processes of writing.

There's a continuum of 'success' within that process, of course: some people can just do it, and some people are beating their heads against a brick wall and might get more out of music, or drawing, or something else entirely but, the basic fact stands, to communicate with others in words is a very human thing; perhaps it is THE human thing; the salient difference between ourselves and the non-linguistic world. And to write that down and share it with others is one hell of a powerful technology. It always has been and it's not going away.

Gandhi said, 'Be the change you want to see in the world' and, whilst I fail in that endeavour a good deal of the time, I find his words a prescient way of thinking about our being here, and for working towards rewarding ways of approaching this confusing business of being. And, as I said before, one of the reasons we read our writers (and one of the reasons we write) is to be changed, and to understand the processes of change that rule our lives. Writing, for me, is the one way I know how best to engage with these processes of change. How could that will to change, and to communicate through writing not be positive; how could we not be optimistic about it?

Maggie Butt

I am very optimistic about the future for writers and writing. The new communication technologies are just vessels, which need content.

Video games, movies, advertising, magazines, the internet, all need writers. Alongside these, technology has not yet superseded the immediacy of the total immersion, of the pictures we get in their heads from reading and listening. It doesn't matter if that's via a book or an electronic device.

The Internet is a much more egalitarian mode of publishing than we've ever had before, and that's great. It means writers can find new audiences, and combine old forms and approaches to make things which are fresh and new. It means readers will have to learn to be more critical, to sift the good from the bad. That can only be good for writing.

Someone told me (I like to think it's true) that poetry and porn are the most searched items on the internet. Not in that order of course, but who knows...

Jack Epps Jr.

My biggest worry is that fewer people are reading today. Reading seems like a lost art. That really concerns me. Reading is something I cherish and do every day. I get up early to read. Reading is like a guilty pleasure – except I don't feel guilty. I have an insatiable curiosity about everything and I can't for the life of me, understand why everyone isn't devouring books to learn more about the wonderful mysteries of our world.

The growth in new methods of communications and media delivery systems, i.e., the internet, should stimulate a growing audience for stories. While reading may be becoming something of a lost art, storytelling and the publics' desire to watch and hear stories are growing. There seems to be fewer opportunities in motion pictures today – fewer films being made – but there are growing opportunities in television due to the growth in cable and satellite programming. Webisodes and other internet sites also offer new means of story delivery. This is sort of a glass half-full, half-empty kind of thing.

The art of storytelling will not die. Homer is just as entertaining today as he has been for centuries. Maybe less people have the patience to read Homer, but the storyteller still has an important role to play in our society. So, I would say. Hang in there. Tell a good story and be true to your instincts.

Nadine Gordimer

I am much concerned about the future of the written word against the image. From nursery school age, people look – don't read, now. The hours in front of the T.V. screen are extended by the portable, including the telephone, telling the existential tale by images, even the spoken work is minor, an accessory ...

Kate Grenville

Humans will always want to tell stories, I think, and use stories to explore the eternal dilemmas and joys of being alive. Whether it's oral stories or pictures on cave walls or poetry or blogs, that urge isn't going to go away. Technology just gives a different way of communicating it – the possibilities of the internet are only just beginning.

Nessa O'Mahony

Yes, I'm very optimistic. People will always have a need to express themselves. Technology might change the shape of that expression, somewhat. I updated my status on Facebook the other day and a friend commented on whether it was the first line of a poem. I wish to goodness it had been, but it gave me a nugget of an idea, all the same.

Ruth Padel

Yes – if they are going to be read. People who 'want to write' without being passionate about reading are digging writing's grave. You can only be as good a writer as you are a reader.

Robert Pinsky

Art is fundamental. The art of poetry, rooted in the human body – see the videos at www.favoritepoem.org – is absolutely fundamental.

Philip Pullman

I feel optimistic about very little. I think we're nearly at the end of human civilization, since quite clearly nothing is going to stop us from devastating the earth and reducing the place to ash and rubble. As for the new forms of communication and so on, the internet is simply too big, there is less genuine choice with 500 TV channels than there was when we only had two, the number of books published is vastly in excess of what we need – there is just too much of everything. We are choking to death on information that says nothing. From time to time – quite frequently, these days – I think it would be a good idea for me to stop producing this stuff myself and adding to the pile. There is enough already.

Tom Shapcott

Yes, my experience at Adelaide University, and the published work of students and ex-students showed me that even in a smallish city/ area there can be a wonderful flowering. In other words, if the talent and the potential are there, the stimulation and incentive can be encouraged. Publication: although there are woes, it is surprising just how many books arising from creative writing Courses do get published. I tend to think of all this as providing a necessary compost, out of which the future health of writing will gain its strength. Just as one of the side-effects of such courses is to provide a more literate, a more responsive, readership (think of the proliferation of reading groups). One of the longer-term results of the University of Adelaide's introduction of creative writing as a course was the increase in the number of informal writing groups, clubs and little cafe sessions. In other words, an interested breeding ground for mutual stimulus and endeavour. A glance at the history of any literary movement, however small, reveals this as a necessary base from which ultimate achievement emerges. I think Australia is lucky, in that you never have to think, 'this has all been done before, and better'; rather there is the sense of everything being possible in the future.

William Tremblay

Are you generally positive about creative writing's present and future in light of the technological advancements such as computers, word processing?

I don't seem to have time for despair. What amazes me right now is how much is going on simultaneously. People have been tolling the death knell of 'serious literature' for decades now, yet more people are doing more kinds of writing than ever.

Obviously the endless need for diversion in terms of television operating '24/7' means that there's a market for all kinds of writing from utter schlock to great works that are moving and brilliantly insightful.

Sometimes this great diversity is going on from the same writer like Stephen King who writes and publishes different kinds of material under pseudonyms like Richard Bachman and John Swithen.

Different people read different kinds of writing for different stages in their personal development. An infinite need creates an infinite opportunity.

I've lived long enough to have thought a range of things as connected such as 'who are you writing for?' I've thought I was writing 'for the people'. I've thought that writing is hope is prayer. I've thought the best thing was to write for the spirit. I've thought the use of poetry and all writing is to make manifest the hidden meanings of human experience. I've thought that poetry is the vehicle of language experiments, i.e. that whatever else poetry is about it's about language. Could it all be true?

I write. I've always written. I'll be at a party, and I'll sit in the kitchen. In the living room, people are dancing. I'll find a bent ballpoint and a scrap of paper. Someone comes into the kitchen, opens the refrigerator for a cold one, then asks, 'Why don't you come dance?' I'll say, 'You dance. I'll write about you dancing. I'll compare your moves to a prairie chicken in mating season. I'm a writer. I write.'

Xu Xi

Oh I'm generally optimistic. I read on a Kindle, and even have read a manuscript on my I-Phone, and I love the greater paper-less-ness new technology allows. I will be even more optimistic if I can work out what the twenty-first century novel will do to trump Modernism, as I don't think we've seen the evolution of the novel in a truly exciting new way comparable to what Woolf and Joyce did (post-modernism is one of those nonsense articulations of theorist who should write less and read more). I do like graphic novels as a form and have much hope for that (*Watchman* is a book I read to the end with no difficulty whatsoever). But I'm generally an optimist, because I have very low expectations of humanity and therefore am rarely disappointed and more often, simply quite surprised and delighted when human endeavour proves me wrong.

* * *

Let's take the less optimistic elements first.

On reflection, there is not an inherent opposition between the word and the image. However, there may well be a problem of engagement, of our *active* reading rather than a *passive* watching, of the contemporary image as a specific challenge to our engagement with certain forms or genre of creative writing. Of course, engaging with images does not have to a passive pastime! But, certain kinds of engagement are more passive than others, and that might be the reason for some concern about the future of the writing arts.

Playing Devil's Advocate, however, it might be argued that the image, spread out logically to embrace all visual representation, *contains* the written word. Thus, what is the problem? Writing is, after all, simply graphic representation. Our concerns for the writing arts are probably more about specific kinds of visual reading, given that we can quickly acknowledge our human predilection for reading the world generally. As creatures, we are indeed readers!

That said, in this chapter both Jack Epps Jr. and Charles Baxter express concern about the number of readers and the future of reading. Nadine Gordimer points directly to 'future of the written word against the image', and picks up on the specific problem of 'telling the existential tale by images'. These comments are a clue to the more specific nature of the challenges faced by certain types of creative writing. . As Kate Grenville says 'humans will always want to tell stories', the specific question might be what we use to tell these stories, and how much creative writing will play its part in that telling. Xu Xi is 'generally optimistic', and mentions the role of new technologies in increasing opportunities for reading. Nessa O'Mahony has a similar technological tale, mentioning: 'I updated my status on Facebook the other day and a friend commented on whether it was the first line of a poem'. However, Philip Pullman comments on information overload, the result also of this twenty-first-century expansion of communication and entertainment technologies. Tom Shapcott comments on the successes arising from creative writing courses, and Andy Brown alludes to other kinds of success in that regard also with his 'job helping people to express themselves in words; how to be better readers; how to write'. Iain Banks strongly suspects 'the novel will survive indefinitely, even if it doesn't represent the cutting edge of narrative technique.'

There's a reasonable balance of opinion among the writers here, perhaps with a (comforting!) tipping towards the side of optimism. Further speculation might have us wondering if in over a century of moving image technologies and around two dozen years of domestic digital communication what we have seen is not just a shift to a more visualised world but a shift to a more *recorded* one. Once recorded the question is what do to with these digital 'objects'. What do we preserve, how do we make those preserved things accessible? Where does the world's constant output of creative writing fit with this preservation? What aspects of creative writing are preserved, by whom, where and how?

The writers in this book clearly display concerns about the future. But their cautious optimism, particularly about the value of the arts, and about the telling of stories, is encouraging. It could be that the writing arts cannot remain the same as they have been in our lifetimes – that they *will* not remain the same. But then, we might ask if they have *ever* remained exactly the same?

One final thought should be reserved for how we aim to recognise the importance of the actions creative writers undertake. Creative Writing is, after all, our creative action firsts, and the results of these actions second. We should think also about how we preserve the objects of creative writing, the variety and extent of such things, how we judge what should be preserved, by whom, when and why..

Reflection

Are you optimistic about the future of creative writing? What makes you optimistic or not optimistic?

As this final chapter/question considered technological change, and the impact on creative writing of new ways of communicating, and interacting, try listing the technologically related things that you do that you feel enhance your creative writing and the things that you do that detract from it. For example, do you benefit from an ease of access to information but find yourself drawn away from writing to attend to some electronically delivered task?

Exercise

Do you feel the writers come to consensus on the questions asked in this book? On all of the questions, on some of them, or on none of them? Can you detect some strands of writerly thought? Try mapping the answers of the creative writers here on each question (suggested length: 100 words per question/answer). For example, how many of the writers mention (in answer to Question 1) that they began writing in childhood; what kinds of things have the writers learnt (in answer to Question 9); in what ways are the writers optimistic or pessimistic about the future of creative writing (in answer to Question 15)?

Conclusion

A conclusion is the place where you got tired of thinking.

Martin Henry Fischer (1879–1962)
Professor of Physiology
University of Cincinnati[1]

The wry Professor Fischer! But this is a well known quote to reach a well known place: a book's conclusion. Placing Fischer's comment to one side, what and where have we reached? Certainly the writers have shared their opinions and in *Inside Creative Writing* we can uniquely compare their answers. The strength in doing this is that you will see, reasonably often, some points of commonality among the writers, and you will also see points of difference.

No two of these writers were asked these questions together, at the same time, so the fact that you will see points of similarity and points of dissimilarity in their answers *is* revealing of how each of the writers individually views creative writing. And a comparative reading of their answers gives you a 'group view'.

Likewise, the aim of the questions in *Inside creative writing* is to focus on the *doing* of creative writing, rather than only the results after it is done. So, in summary, Question 1 is about starting creative writing, Question 2 is about the influence of other people, at that starting point, and Question 3 is about the passion for doing it. In Question 4 we look at whether the 'creative' in creative writing might occupy a writer's mind, while in Question 5 and Question 6 we look at the practicalities of developing work from start to finish. Question 7 asks whether the writers share their efforts, before they are done, in some ways asking if the writers have 'sounding bounds' to assist them along the way. In Question 9 it is the place and time of writing that is the focus, the writers' habitats. Questions 10 and 11 are about knowledge – 'thinking' knowledge and 'acting' knowledge, we might say, 'art' knowledge and 'craft' knowledge. The focus of Question 12 is essentially the 'anything else that to you that you feel is practically significant', with an emphasis on how the writers *actually* work. Questions 13 and 14 are about demonstration and questioning – an activity and questions for other writers. Question 15 rounds up with a look towards a creative writing future.

Incidentally, in addition to wry comment our opening 'quotee', Martin Henry Fischer, is also responsible for declaring: 'research has been called good business, a necessity, a gamble, a game. It is none of these – it's a state of mind'.[2] Perhaps our thoughts here should also be about that 'state of mind' we have reached through the research in *Inside creative writing*. Certainly we can see much in comparing and contrasting the responses of the creative writers in this book. Comparisons yield evidence. Evidence gives us substance, important material, to explore.

If we consider where there are similarities and differences in the writers' responses we can see patterns of thinking, and we can speculate (because we cannot observe them writing 'live') about the patterns of their actions, their activities of creative writing. We can, likewise, detect in their responses their personal feelings, their individual dispositions (or temperaments). We can consider how our own thoughts and creative writing actions compare to the answers given by these creative writers.

Yet still we have to ask: where does this leave us?

There is no fixed table of action to refer to here, no 'how to' training manual for creative writing that if followed as a creative writers' bible of practice will instantly make you a creative writer. Even technical skill is never understood in the same way by every writer – though particular technical questions can certainly be explored further, and some of the exercises in the preceding chapters focus on technique or, more broadly speaking, on the practical actions involved in undertaking creative writing.

Questions about drafting, about the knowledge that writers draw upon and develop, link to our individual our 'internal' decision making, moving from our personal ideas or emotions or observations to the actual activities of creative writing. For many creative writers, the word 'creative' does not particularly suggest ways of doing things, but it does suggest a predisposition. In that sense, the creative is located on the *inside* of our activities. The role of what might be called our 'situated individuality' in the actions of creative writing is significant. You, as a creative writer, working within a culture, in the context of your relationships with others, and in relation to your personal circumstances.

A creative writer might frequently treat the matter of 'practicalities' as something of a 'what works for me' situation, but there is also a sense that what is behind these individual practices is what one of the creative writers here calls 'instinct' or 'instincts'. Can such instincts be developed or honed in ourselves or in others? That is a question anyone learning or teaching creative writing must surely ask themselves. One thing is for sure, a passion for *doing* creative writing is essential. It is no surprise that some of the creative writers here openly comment that they 'love it' or 'can't imagine going through life without it'.

Creative writing is naturally not unique in the world in that melding of love and labour. But what is unique about creative writing is the tools that are used, the formation of art and communication through the creative use of words. This involves our relationship with particularised combinations of knowledge. We learn things by doing creative writing that we might not have otherwise known, or even sought to know. Creative writing knowledge ('situational knowledge' as I've called it) is bound to the writing work-at-hand. A key value of this knowledge is its role in creating personal exchanges, its bridging between one individual and another, its alerting others to ideas or emotions and to ways of interpreting what is around them. This value of creative writing is bound up in the important role of feelings in our human world, those slippery human responses that don't just come from an application of the mind, or the arrangement of facts. The kind of truth this knowledge employs, the value it has, and the ways in which it is shared, is worthy of our further exploration. The reflections and exercises in this book provide some assistance for undertaking these explorations.

Though some of the creative writers here perceive the existence of threats to the future of creative writing, the optimism connected with a confidence in the significance of the arts in human life is nothing short of celebratory. Our widespread engagement with storytelling, our development of new forms of delivering of creative writing (for example, the emergence of new reading technologies) and again our general passion for undertaking creative writing. Each of these also offers some directions towards the future. Creative writing might not always be a sure thing but our belief in it, and desire to practice it, our willingness to spend time and energy doing it, reflects creative writing's importance.

Few of the writers in this book ponder on how other creative writers undertake their creative writing. Their own undertakings more often fill much of their time. Even if an individual writer shares with friends, an editor or publisher, or writes in a partnership, they nevertheless proceed on the basis of creative writing as their own, something others might do but something that they do personally. This is undoubtedly another meaning of those words *Inside Creative Writing*.

The writers: biographic snapshots

What follows are snapshots, my personal brief introductions to the writers interviewed here. These are entirely my own pointers, and there are gaps in them – for example, many of these writers have won considerable awards for their work, but I have not mentioned many all these, and I have not included all the writers' works either.

Creative writing is so widely undertaken, and so widely enjoyed here in the twenty-first century that a simple web search will reveal much more about any of these writers than could ever be included in any one biographical note. Of course, I have made the point that this book is not about fame, it is about creative writing. The two do have a relationship, but they are very far from the same thing. Some creative writers will become famous because of their writing (some will become famous or infamous for other reasons!). A great many creative writers will not ever reach any level of fame, whatsoever, yet their engagement with creative writing will be as lively and as human as anyone else's.

I have noted previously that what holds these writers together as a 'case study' is that they have all had some external involvement in their final works, some publishing or producing involvement, but in many ways the most important thing is that they are a group of people who write.

* * *

Iain Banks

Someone who primarily moves between the writing of fiction and the writing of science fiction, distinctively publishing as Iain Banks when publishing fiction and Iain M. Banks when publishing science fiction. Iain was born in Scotland in 1954. Works include *The Wasp Factory* (1984), *Espedair Street* (1987), *The Crow Road* (1992), *Feersum Endjinn* (1994), *Look to Windward* (2000), *Dead Air* (2002), *The Steps to Garbadale* (2007), *Surface Detail* (2010) and many others.

Charles Baxter

A writer of fiction, non-fiction and poetry. Born in Minneapolis, Minnesota, USA in 1947. He holds a PhD in English from the University of Buffalo, began his teaching career at Wayne State University, and most recently has been Edelstein-Keller Professor in creative writing at the University of Minnesota. Some of his works are *First Light* (1987), *Imaginary Paintings and Other Poems* (1989), *A Relative Stranger* (1990), *Shadow Play* (1993), *Burning Down the House* (1997), *The Feast of Love* (2000), *Saul and Patsy* (2003), *Beyond Plot* (2007) and *The Soul Thief* (2008)

Andy Brown

Born in the United Kingdom in 1966. Poet and Director of the Centre for Creative Writing & Arts at the University of Exeter, Andy also writes short stories and criticism and his reviews (particularly of poetry) are widely published. Some of his works include *The Sleep Switch* (1996), *West of Yesterday* (1998), *From A Cliff* (2002), *The Trust*

Territory (2005), *The Storm Berm* (2008) and *Goose Music* (2008), with John Burnside.

Maggie Butt

Maggie is currently Chair of the UK's National Association of Writers in Education (NAWE). A poet, she has also been head of the Media Department and the Skillset Media Academy at Middlesex University, among other university posts. Having worked as a documentary writer, producer and director she returned to poetry after some time away from it, and also holds a PhD in creative writing from Cardiff University in Wales. Her works include *Lipstick* (2007), *petite* (2010), and *Ally Pally Prison Camp* (2011).

Jack Epps Jr.

A screenwriter and producer, Jack was born in 1949 in Detroit, USA. Much of his work in the later part of the twentieth century was undertaken with writing partner Jim Cash (1941–2000). Those film writing works include *Legal Eagles* (1986), *Top Gun* (1989), *Turner and Hooch* (1989), also with Dennis Shyrack, Michael Blodgett and Daniel Petrie Jr., *Dick Tracy* (1990), *Anaconda* (1997), also with Hans Bauer, and *The Flintstones in Viva Rock Vegas* (2000), also with Deborah Kaplan and Harry Elfont. His work also appears on the TV Series, *Hawaii Five-0* (1968–1980) and *Kojak* (1973–1978).

Nadine Gordimer

Nadine Gordimer's first works included *Face to Face* (1949) and *The Lying Days* (1953). She was born in 1923 in Springs, a city not far from Johannesburg, South Africa. Her involvement in the anti-apartheid movement, and her work against censorship and state control of the literary arts has been considerable, and has been Vice-President of the International PEN. Nadine Gordimer was awarded the Nobel Prize for Literature in 1991, this among her many other awards and honours. Her works of creative writing are many, and include *Occasion for Loving* (1963), *The Conservationist* (1974), *Burger's Daughter* (1979), *A Soldier's Embrace* (1980), *Something Out There* (1984), *My Son's Story* (1990), *Jump and Other Stories* (1991), *The House Gun* (1998), *Loot and Other Stories* (2003), *Get a Life* (2005) and *Beethoven Was One Sixteenth Black* (2007).

Kate Grenville

Kate Grenville was born in 1950 in Sydney, Australia. A novelist and short story writer, her published works include *Sarah Thornhill* (2011), *The Lieutenant* (2008), *Searching for the Secret River* (2006), *The Secret River* (2005), *Writing from Start to Finish: A Six Step Guide* (2001), *The Idea of Perfection* (1999) *Dark Places* (1994), *The Writing Book: A Manual for Fiction Writers* (1990), *Joan Makes History: A Novel* (1988) and *Bearded Ladies* (1984). She once worked in the film industry, and also holds degrees in creative writing: a Masters degree from the University of Colorado at Boulder and a Doctor of Creative Arts degree from the University of Technology, Sydney. www.kategrenville.com

Nessa O'Mahony

Nessa was born in Dublin in 1964. She currently lives in Dublin. Nessa is a poet, editor and reviewer. She holds a Masters degree in creative writing from the University of East Anglia and a Doctorate in Creative and Critical Writing from Bangor University, Wales. Associate Editor of the literary journal *Orbis*, she has also been the artist in residence at the John Hume Institute for Global Irish Studies at University College Dublin, and recipient of literary bursary from Arts Council of Ireland / An Chomhairle Éalaíon. Her works include *Trapping a Ghost* (2007) and *In Sight of Home* (2009), among others, and she has published her poetry widely in magazines and journals.

Ruth Padel

Ruth Padel's works include *Alibi* (1985), *In and Out of the Mind: Greek Images of the Tragic Self* (1992), *Fusewire* (1996), *52 Ways of Looking at a Poem: Or How Reading Modern Poetry Can Change Your Life* (2002), *Voodoo Shop* (2002), *The Soho Leopard* (2004), *Tigers in Red Weather* (2005), *A Darwin: A Life in Poems* (2009) and *Where the Serpents Live* (2010). The titles of these works perhaps give some indication already of the range of Ruth's work; but, to bring up that point, these examples cover collections of poetry, works of literary criticism, fiction and a travel memoir. Perhaps most known as a poet, Ruth Padel was Chair of the Poetry Society from 2004 to 2006. She was born in London in 1946.

Robert Pinsky

Former United States Poet Laureate and Consultant in Poetry to the Library of Congress, Robert Pinsky founded the Favourite Poem Project, 'dedicated to celebrating, documenting and encouraging poetry's role in Americans' lives'. He holds an MA and a PhD in Philosophy from Stanford University, and has taught for some time in the writing programme at Boston University. He is a critic and translator as well as a poet, and he was born in Long Branch, New Jersey, in 1940. Among his many works are included *Sadness and Happiness* (1975), *The Situation of Poetry* (1977), *History of My Heart* (1984), *The Inferno of Dante: A New Verse Translation* (1995), *Jersey Rain* (2000), *Democracy, Culture, and the Voice of Poetry* (2002) and *Gulf Music: Poems* (2007).

Philip Pullman

Philip Pullman's many books for children and for adults include *Count Karlstein* (1982), *The Ruby in the Smoke* (1985), *The Broken Bridge* (1990), *The Firework-Maker's Daughter* (1995), *The Gasfitter's Ball* (1995); the trilogy *His Dark Materials*, beginning *Northern Lights* (1995 – and entitled *The Golden Compass* in the USA), *The Subtle Knife* (1997), and ending with *The Amber Spyglass* (2000); *The Scarecrow and His Servant* (2004) and *The Good Man Jesus and the Scoundrel Christ* (2010). He was born in Norwich in 1946, and educated in England, Zimbabwe, Australia and North Wales. He taught for a number of years in schools around Oxford, then later on a Bachelor of Education course – though he notes on his personal website, that 'my views on education are eccentric and unimportant, however. My only real claim to anyone's attention lies in my writing.' Attention and enthusiastic interest, from both children and adults, has certainly been forthcoming, and his published works have also found their way onto television and the stage and into film. www.philip-pullman.com

Tom Shapcott

Tom has written poetry, novels and short stories, libretti, dramas and dance pieces, criticism, and works for children. He has also been known to many in his other public roles as Director of the Literature Board of the Australia Council (1983–1990), Executive Director of the National Book Council (1991–1997), and as inaugural Professor of creative writing at the University of Adelaide (1997–2005). Born in Ipswich, Queensland, in 1935, and beginning his formal working life as an accountant – and, indeed, establishing his own accountancy firm in 1972 – he later became a full-time writer, notwithstanding the public roles he has frequently occupied. His works, the largest number of which are works of poetry, include *The City of Empty Rooms* (2006), *Adelaide Lunch Sonnets* (2006), *Spirit Wrestlers* (2004), *Music Circus and Other Poems* (2004), *Chekhov's Mongoose* (2000), *Search for Galina* (1990), *The Art of Charles Blackman* (1989), *White Stag of Exile* (1985), *The Birthday Gift* (1982), *Begin with Walking* (1973) and *Inwards to the Sun* (1969).

William Tremblay

William (Bill) Tremblay is poet, novelist, editor, a regular reviewer and a teacher. *Rainstorm over the Alphabet: Poems 1990–2000* (2005) and *Shooting Script: Door of Fire* (2003) are good places to start to explore his work. Born in Southbridge, Massachusetts in 1940, he is an emeritus professor at Colorado State University, where he taught from 1973 onwards. His poems have been widely published in journals and anthologies and his first novel *The June Rise: The Apocryphal Letters of Joseph Antoine Janis* was published by Utah State University Press in 1994. Other works include, though this is not of course a full list: *Crying in the Cheap Seats* (1971), *The Anarchist HeartHome FrontColorado Review* member of the Program Directors Council of the Associated Writing Programs (AWP).

Xu Xi

Xu Xi's works include Chinese Walls (1994), Daughters of Hui (1996), Hong Kong Rose (1997), The Unwalled City (2001), History's Fiction (2001), Overleaf Hong Kong (2004), Evanescent Isles: From My City-Village (2008) and Habitat of a Foreign Sky: A Novel (2010). Born in 1954, her website describes her as being 'of reluctant fixed abode' and she makes note of her travels between New York, New Zealand and Hong Kong. She holds a Master of Fine Arts (MFA) degree in fiction writing from the University of Massachusetts at Amherst and she currently teaches in the international low-residency MFA programme at the City University of Hong Kong. She has also recently edited Fifty-Fifty: New Hong Kong Writing (2010), an anthology of new writing from 43 Hong Kong writers, and focusing on the present and future of Hong Kong as a 'special administrative region' (SAR) of the People's Republic of China, autonomous from mainland China until 2047 under a principle known as 'one country, two systems'.

Notes

Introduction

1. The definition of acts and actions used here is: Actions are 'a collection of acts, sometimes joined by logic, intuition or fortuitous circumstance'. An act is 'something done'.
2. Using the word *signifier* here in a general sense, and in straightforward terms, based on the distinction made by linguist, Ferdinand de Saussure (1857–1913), that 'each sign in language is a union of signifier (i.e. a sound image or its graphic equivalent) and a signified (i.e. the referent; the concept referred to)' in J.A. Cuddon, *Dictionary of Literary Terms and Literary Theory*, London: Penguin, 1991, p. 879.
3. Jane Piirto, 'The Personalities of Creative Writers', in Scott Barry Kaufman and James C. Kaufman, eds, *The Psychology of Creative Writing*, New York: Cambridge University Press, 2009, p. 3.
4. Scott Barry Kaufman and James C. Kaufman, eds, *The Psychology of Creative Writing*, New York: Cambridge University Press, 2009, p. 369.
5. C.E. Seashore. 'The Inheritance of Musical Talent', *The Musical Quarterly*, Vol. 6, No. 4 (Oct., 1920), p. 586. pp. 586–598.
6. Edwin G. Flemming, 'Personality and Artistic Talent', *Journal of Educational Sociology*, Vol. 8, No. 1 (Sep., 1934), p. 27. pp. 27–33.
7. Michael Pickering and Keith Negus, 'Rethinking Creative Genius', *Popular Music*, Vol. 23, No. 2 (May, 2004), p. 202. pp. 198–203.
8. Rollo May, *The Courage to Create*, New York: Norton, 1975, p. 39.
9. John White, 'Creativity', in David Cooper, ed., *A Companion to Aesthetics*, Oxford: Blackwell, 1995.
10. George Bailey in David Cooper, ed., *A Companion to Aesthetics*, Oxford: Blackwell, 1995, p. 316.

2   Creative Writers and Others

1. 'According to Collingwood, each act of the imagination has an impression, or sensuous experience, at its base, which by mental activity is converted into an idea' in Gordon Graham, *Philosophy of the Arts: An Introduction to Aesthetics*, London: Routledge, p. 32.
2. Graeme Harper, 'Creative Benefaction', *New Writing: the International Journal for the Practice and Theory of Creative Writing*, Vol. 7, No. 2, Abington: Taylor and Francis, 2010, p. 1.

3. Arthur S. Reber, *Dictionary of Psychology,* London: Penguin, 1985, p. 360.

3   Passions for Creative Writing

1. Frank Conroy, ed., 'Introduction', *The Eleventh Draft: Craft and the Writing Life from the Iowa Writers' Workshop,* New York: Harper Collins, 1999, p. xii.
2. Daniel Nettle, 'The Evolution of Creative Writing', in Scott Barry Kaufmann and James C Kaufmann, eds, *The Psychology of Creative Writing,* New York: Cambridge University Press, 2009, p. 109.
3. Ingmar Bergman, 'What is Making Films', in Andrew Sarris, *Interviews with Film Directors*, New York: Avon, 1967, p. 44 – reprinted from *Cahiers du Cinema*, No. 61, July 1956.
4. Odysseus Elytis in Donald Friedman, ed., *The Writer's Brush: Paintings, Drawings and Sculptures by Writers*, Minneapolis: Mid-List, 2007, p. 120.
5. Dorothea Brande, *Becoming A Writer*, London: Macmillan, 1996, first published 1934, p. 34.

4   That Word 'Creative'

1. Rob Pope, *Creativity: Theory, History, Practice*, London: Routledge, 2005, p. 1.
2. Mihaly Csikszentmihalyi, *Creativity: Flow and the Psychology of Discovery and Invention*, New York: Harper Perennial, 1997, p. 23.

6   Other Creative Writers

1. Seamus Heaney, *The Place of Writing,* Atlanta: Scholars Press, 1989.
2. Heaney, p. 2.
3. Heaney, p. 51.
4. Heaney, p. 25.

8   Creative Writing Habitats

1. See Graeme Harper, 'Creative Habitats and the Creative Domain', *New Writing: The International Journal for the Practice and Theory of Creative Writing*, Vol. 7, No. 1, (Spring 2010), p. 1.

9   Knowledge: Subjects and Themes

1. The expression 'justified true belief' is a well discussed expression. Many will point to Plato's *Theaetetus* (a recent published version is:

Plato, *Theaetetus*, Joe Sachs trans., Newburyport: Focus, 2010) and the dialogue there concerning differences between belief and knowledge, the role of judgement and the role of perception.

10 Writing Craft and Skills

1. Comment by David Revere McFadden, Chief Curator and Vice President, Museum of Arts & Design, New York, on the V&A web page entitled 'What is Craft?' Victoria and Albert Museum, London. Stated in the V&A's introduction to this page: 'To celebrate a new partnership between the V&A and the Crafts Council, we asked leading figures in the craft world to tell us what the term craft means to them'. http://www.vam.ac.uk/collections/contemporary/crafts/what_is_craft/index.html Last accessed 30 October 2010
2. Ference Marton, 'Skill as an Aspect of Knowledge', *The Journal of Higher Education*, Vol. 50, No. 5 (1979), pp. 602–614.

12 Other Practicalities

1. Jane Grayson, *Vladimir Nabokov*, New York: Overlook, 2001.
2. Mihaly Csikszentmihalyi, *Creativity: Flow and the Psychology of Discovery and Invention*, New York: Harper, 1997, p. 95.
3. Csikszentmihalyi, p. 87.

13 Exploring Creative Writing Exercises

1. James Gunn, 'Can Creative Writing Be Taught?' *Mississippi Review*, Vol. 19, No. 1/2, Workshops (1990), p. 303.
2. Mathew Brennan, 'Can Writing Be Taught?' *Mississippi Review*, Vol. 19, No. 1/2, Workshops (1990), p. 295.
3. Kendra Kopelke, 'Can Writing Be Taught?' *Mississippi Review*, Vol. 19, No. 1/2, Workshops (1990), p. 308.
4. Kevin Volans, 'Dancing in the Dark: Craft and Composition', *Circa*, No. 47, The Craft Issue (Sep.–Oct., 1989), p. 18.
5. Volans, p. 20.

14 Asking Another Writer a Question

1. Jon Frederickson and James F. Rooney, *International Review of the Aesthetics and Sociology of Music, How the Music Occupation Failed to Become a Profession*, Vol. 21, No. 2, 1990, p. 190.
2. Frederickson and Rooney, p. 203.
3. Jack Kerouac, interviewed by Ted Berrigan, 'The Art of Fiction No. 41', *The Paris Review* (Summer 1968), No. 43.

4. Les Murray, interviewed by Dennis O'Driscoll, 'The Art of Poetry No. 89', *The Paris Review* (Spring 2005), No. 173.
5. Robert Penn Warren, interviewed by Eugene Walter and Ralph Ellison, 'The Art of Fiction No. 18, *The Paris Review* (Spring-Summer 1957), No. 16.
6. Elliot J. Gorn, 'The Historians' Dilemma', *The Journal of American History*, Vol. 90, No. 4 (Mar., 2004), p. 1330.
7. Gorn, p. 1332.
8. Paul Muldoon, *The End of the Poem*, New York: Farrar, Strauss and Giroux, 2006, p. 299
9. Muldoon, p. 361.
10. Ernest Hemingway, interviewed by George Plimpton, The Art of Fiction No.21, *The Paris Review* (Spring 1958), No. 18.

Conclusion

1. Smith Dent, ed., 'Fischerisms', *Encore: A Continuing Anthology*, 1945, p. 309.
2. Howard Fabing and Ray Marr, eds, *Fischerisms*, Springfield,Il & Baltimore, Md. Charles C. Thomas, A Private Print for His Students, 1937.

Further Reading

Allott, Miriam, *Novelists on the Novel*, London: Routledge, 1973.

Arana, Maria, ed., *The Writing Life: Writers on How They Think and Work*, New York: Public Affairs, 2003.

Atwood, Margaret, *Negotiating with the Dead: A Writer on Writing*, Cambridge: Cambridge University Press, 2002.

Auster, Paul, *The Art of Hunger*, London: Faber, 1998.

Baron, Dennis *A Better Pencil: Readers, Writers, and the Digital Revolution*, Oxford: Oxford University Press, 2009.

Barth, John, *Letters: A Novel*, London: Secker and Warburg, 1980.

Barthelme, Donald, *The Teachings of Donald B.*, Kim Herzinger, ed., New York: Vintage, 1998.

Blotner, Joseph, ed., *Selected Letters of William Faulkner*, New York: Random House, 1977.

Boylan, Clare, *The Agony and the Ego: The Art and Strategy of Fiction Writing Explored*, Penguin: London, 1993.

Cheever, John, *The Journals of John Cheever*, New York: Knopf, 1991.

Chekhov, Anton, *The Selected Letters of Anton Chekhov*, Lillian Hellman, ed., London: Picador, 1988.

Cole, Toby, *Playwrights on Playwriting*, New York: Hill and Wang, 1988.

Conroy, Frank, *The Eleventh Draft: Craft and Writing Life form the Iowa Writers Workshop*, New York: Harper Collins, 1999.

Darnton, John, *Writers on Writing: Collected Essays from The New York Times*, NY: Holt, 2001.

Day-Lewis, Cecil, *The Poet's Way of Knowledge*, Cambridge: CUP, 1957.

Edel, Leon and Lyall H Powers, eds, *The Complete Notebooks of Henry James*, New York: OUP, 1988.

Evans, Mari, ed., *Black Women Writers: Arguments and Interviews*, London: Pluto, 1985.

Fitzgerald, Sally, ed., *The Habit of Being: The Letters of Flannery O'Connor*, New York: Vintage, 1979.

Friedman, Donald, *The Writer's Brush: Paintings, Drawings and Sculpture by Writers*, Minneapolis: Mid-List, 2007.

Fugard, Athol, *Notebooks of Athol Fugard: 1960–1977*, Mary Benson, ed., London: Faber, 1983.

Gardner, John, *The Art of Fiction: Notes on Craft for Young Writers*, New York: Vintage, 1991.

Ginsburg, Allen, *Indian Journals: Notebooks, Diaries, Blank Pages, Writings*, London: Penguin, 1990.

Grass, Gunter, *On Writing and Politics: 1967–1983*, San Diego: Harcourt, 1985.

Grayson, Jane, *Vladimir Nabokov*, Woodstock: Overlook, 2001.

Harper, Graeme, *New Writing: The International Journal for the Practice and Theory of Creative Writing*, Abingdon: Routledge.

Henry, DeWitt, *Breaking into Print: Early Stories and Insights into Getting Published*, Boston: Beacon, 2000.

Hesse, Hermann, *Autobiographical Writings*, London: Picador, 1973.

Hughes, Ted, *Poetry in the Making: A Handbook for Writing and Teaching*, London: Faber, 2008, first published 1968.

Johns, Adrian, *The Nature of the Book: Print and Knowledge in the Making*, Chicago: University of Chicago Press, 1998.

Le Guin, Ursula K., *Steering the Craft: Exercises and Discussions on Story Writing for the Lone Navigator or the Mutinous Crew*, Portland: The Eighth Mountain Press, 1998.

Le Guin, Ursula K., *The Wave in the Mind: Talks on the Writer, the Reader and the Imagination*. Shambala, Boston, 2004.

Levi, Primo, *The Mirror Maker: Stories and Essays*, New York: Schocken, 1989.

Manguel, Alberto, *A History of Reading*, London: Harper Collins, 1996.

Marquez, Gabriel Garcia, *Living to Tell the Tale*, New York: Vintage, 2004.

Marr, David, *Patrick White: A Life*, Sydney: Vintage, 1992.

Moore, Marianne, interviewed by Donald Hall, *The Paris Review*, Issue 26, Summer-Fall, 1961.

Morrison, Toni, What *Moves at the Margin: Selected Nonfiction*, Carolyn C. Denard, ed., Jackson: University of Mississippi, 2008.

Motion, Andrew, *Philip Larkin: A Writer's Life*, London: Faber, 1994.

Naipaul, V.S., Reading *and Writing: A Personal Account*, New York: New York Review of Books, 2000.

Nin, Anaïs, *The Novel of the Future*, Athens; Ohio University Press, 1986.

Oates, Joyce Carol, *Uncensored: Views and Reviews*, New York: Harper, 2005.

Oldfield, Sybil, *Afterwords: Letters on the Death of Virginia Woolf*, Edinburgh; Edinburgh University Press, 2005.

Ozick, Cynthia, *Quarrel and Quandary*, New York: Knopf, 2000.

Phillips, Larry, ed., *F. Scott Fitzgerald on Writing*, NY: Scribner, 1988.

Phillips, Larry, ed., *Ernest Hemingway on Writing*, NY: Scribner, 2004.

Pope, Rob, *Creativity: Theory, History, Practice*, London: Routlege, 2005.

Pritchett, V.S., *Midnight Oil*, London: Penguin, 1974.

Proust, Marcel, *Selected Letters: 1880–1903*, Chicago: University of Chicago Press, 1998.

Schwarz, Ronald B., ed., *For the Love of Books: 115 Celebrated Writers on the Books they Most Love*, New York: Berkeley, 2000.

Sullivan, Ceri and Graeme Harper, eds, *Authors at Work: The Creative Environment*, Cambridge: Brewer, 2009.

Thomas, Dylan, *Dylan Thomas: The Collected Letters*, Paul Ferris, ed., London: Paladin, 1987.

Thwaite, Anthony, *Selected Letters of Philip Larkin: 1940–1985*, London: Faber, 1992.

Updike, John, interviewed by Charles Thomas Samuels, *The Paris Review*, Issue 45, Winter 1968.

Vargas Llosa, Mario, *A Writer's Reality*, London; Faber, 1991.

Vonnegut, Kurt, *A Man Without a Country*, New York: Random House, 2005.

Wandor, Michelene *The Author Is Not Dead, Merely Somewhere Else*: *Creative Writing Reconceived*, Basingstoke: Palgrave Macmillan, 2008.

Welty, Eudora, interviewed by Linda Kuehl, *The Paris Review*, Issue 55, Fall 1972.

White, Edmund, *Arts and Letters,* San Francisco: Cleis, 2004.

Woolf, Virginia, *Between the Acts*, London: Grafton, 1978, first published 1941.

Index